READY, SET, GROW!

MAKE MORE MONEY AND KEEP IT

ROY NEWEY

Publishing in the United Kingdom by Roy Newey

Written by Roy Newey
roy@roynewey.com
www.roynewey.com

Graphics created by Olivia Newey, Annie Giorgobia,
Editors: Sam Newey, Olivia Newey and Davene Wasser
Book design & layout by Velin@Perseus-Design.com

ISBN Number:
978-1-64970-690-4 (Paperback)
978-1-64970-687-4 (Ebook)

TABLE OF CONTENTS

· ·

PREFACE

· · · · · · · · · · ·

This book presents a system I developed, to enable businesses of all sizes to plan for accelerated, sustainable and profitable growth. Over the last 40 years, I have developed this system to help my clients and companies accelerate the growth in their businesses and now I am sharing it with you. This book outlines each step in the system you need to take to optimize successful growth. Each chapter takes you through the system to build the growth/implementation action plan, which ends with a recap of the 10 simple golden tips to improve your business. It is proven to accelerate the growth of your business for sustainable profits and if you follow it fully it will ensure success. I have used these tools to grow each of my own businesses and supported hundreds of other business owners to drive the accelerated growth of their companies. The contents of this book are not wishful ideas or concepts, they are real, battle proven, practical tools which you can use – starting today.

Throughout my career I have received so much wonderful advice on how to improve my leadership and businesses and I am forever grateful to the many generous people who gave me their time and ideas. Now it is my turn to give back. As you read, take advantage of this accumulated advice to build a substantial action plan and take your business to the next level.

The book does not seek to address every issue you will face, but the 120 golden tips and 12 detailed chapters will provide significant insight on the practical steps you can take to remove risk and increase the likelihood of achieving business success. I do not, however, want this to just to be an instruction manual, I want it to be a workbook. I have provided a page at the end of each chapter for you to record the three key learning points you have taken from the chapter to start your journey towards accelerating your business growth.

To make the most out of this book, read each chapter, review the tips and then take a moment to start developing your unique action plan, inputting the advice and steps from each chapter so it becomes a working plan. By the end of the book, you should have created your own personalised growth plan. You can then share it with a few trusted sources; friends, mentors, partners, ask for their honest feedback and improve your plan. You will have a detailed, final plan which you can immediately start implementing to achieve accelerated, sustainable and profitable growth.

Congratulations on taking this first step to achieve your financial goals. These tools have served me well over the last 40 years – tools I am still using today and now they will serve you.

HOW TO GET THE MOST OUT OF THIS BOOK

· ·

Thank you for purchasing this book. To secure the most value out of the system for accelerating your growth and sustainable profits in this book, I recommend:

- Read through each chapter thoroughly with a pencil in hand to make notes as you go
- Highlight ideas, suggestions and examples which are meaningful for you and your business
- Review the ten golden tips at the end of each chapter
- Write down three key learning points you want to remember at the end of each chapter
- Complete the 6 action points at the end of each chapter - identify a person to lead and a clear deadline for completion
- Photocopy the 12 completed action plans and bind them together to create a collection of:

o 36 Key Learning Points
o 120 Golden Tips
o 72 Action Points

- Throughout the book you will see small examples of diagrams, templates and tools visit my website www.roynewey.com to download resources, templates, action plans, case studies and additional information.
- Visit my website www.roynewey.com and sign up for a one-month free membership of the **Ready, Set, Grow! Online Club**. This club has monthly meetings, webinars, email support, quarterly meetings and 1:1 support to implement and drive the system set out in this book in your business.
- On-line resources:
  - o A free monthly **Book Club** where we review a business book together online and develop a deeper understanding of the concepts and how we can utilise them in our businesses.
  - o Sign up for my **Ready, Set, Grow! Online Club**. We have monthly meetings, webinars, email support, quarterly meetings and 1:1 support to drive the system set out in this book through your business.
  - o Sign up for my **Leadership Mountaineers Club**. This monthly club is focused on the senior team in a business and tackles leadership issues, includes guest speakers, case studies, debates and quarterly meetings.
  - o Sign up for my **Young Leadership Mountaineers Club**. This monthly club is focused on younger leadership team members, perhaps as part of a family business succession strategy. The focus will be how to step into a leadership role and confidently make an impact.

- Contact me at roy@roynewey.com and book a free zoom call to discuss any issues contained within the book and how they relate to your business.
- Contact me at roy@roynewey.com for further email support as you take advantage of the ideas in this book to accelerate the growth of growth and sustainable profits of your business.

This book is a small way of thanking Sam, Olivia and Tom for all of their love and support whilst I indulged in business. At every step of my business career I have been sustained and re-energized by my family. Thank you for keeping my feet firmly on the ground. I also want to thank all of the mentors, coaches and trainers who have so generously passed on their insights, words of wisdom and tips. Every day I continue to learn from the path that others have taken.

In chapter two we will consider the importance of knowing your WHY. It is critical that businesses are driven by leaders who are clear about their WHY. So, I thought it would be helpful to set out my WHY for writing this book. Over the last 40 years I have made many mistakes and learnt from them. I have worked with some amazing people in 85 countries around the world who taught me many different lessons about leadership, entrepreneurialism, strategy and energy. I know my business life has been enhanced through this patchwork of knowledge. I want the business leaders of today and tomorrow to have the opportunity to pick up this book and benefit from a sample of the lessons I have learnt over the last 40 years. This book does not contain all the answers, but it does contain many nuggets which will enable you to shorten your learning cycle. Put them to good use and share your success.

Good Luck,
Roy

1

LET'S START AT THE BEGINNING

· · · · · · · · · · · · · · · · ·

When I was 10 years old, I persuaded my parents to rent an allotment for me to grow vegetables. I signed up the local corner shop to sell my lettuce on a sale-or-return basis. Each day after school, I would run down to the corner shop to see how many lettuces had been sold so that I could rush back to my allotment and harvest the next crop. If I sold two lettuces a day, I was ecstatic. My career as a serial entrepreneur was set. It was only many years later that I recalled eating a lot of salad as a child and hearing my siblings complain to my Mum, that they were going to turn into lettuces, when I realised the truth. I suspect my Mum was the only person buying my lettuce from the local corner shop.

My path over the next few years was not a straight one, nor one that was particularly linked, but it is what has allowed me to acquire the knowledge I have today. After school I set my sights on owning a restaurant and at 24 years of age, I achieved this goal. I subsequently opened a coffee shop, bakery, florist and wholesale butchers. After several national awards I felt I had achieved my childhood dream and I needed a bigger canvas on which to paint the rest of my story. My next venture was the opportunity to lead a chunk of economic regeneration in Merseyside, where I learned from community leaders, senior members of the private sector and government officials how energies and funding could be aligned to drive the economic growth of a city region. Seven wonderful years in this role gave me a passion for improving people's lives and led to an invitation to invest in a company and take this mission to the next stage. I grabbed it with both hands. It was a role to innovate, build and create solutions for communities and grow the business as a whole. In doing this, I led its expansion internationally, entering into 15 countries and undertaking consultancy in 85 countries. During this period, I was invited to join the boards of several companies who wanted to accelerate their growth. In this role I was able to refine my system for driving growth. After a successful sale and exit from my own business, I decided to use the knowledge, contacts and portfolio I had built up to start a consultancy business. With this knowledge set, I have driven growth in over 100 companies, organisations, non-profits and governmental bodies as a board member, chairman, executive director or business coach.

I am not an academic scholar; I have enjoyed success as a business owner and leader and I now want to share this system for accelerating your growth and sustainable profits. My opportunities, posts and adventures have allowed me to hone my knowledge and create a system, tried and tested by me around the world, to accelerate growth and maintain sustainable profits of a business. The system is in this book and I am now sharing it with you.

Be Careful What You Wish For......

I often get asked to help business owners grow their business. They want a silver bullet or a magic wand. They want a single dose of business growth medicine to cure all their ills and grow their business. My answer is a simple one; you can grow your business, if you follow my tried and tested system. But, be very careful what you wish for...

There are lots of other exciting things to do with your time, passion and energy than set up and run a successful business. Running a business will never be a walk in the park. Running a business will be tough and you will need to prepare yourself for a bumpy ride. There will be long hours, working at weekends, worries about customers, staff, suppliers and cashflow. Your relationships at home, with friends and at work will be stretched to their limits and you can look forward to many sleepless nights, missed holidays and no social time, so go into this with your eyes open. But there will also be successes and celebrations along the way and if you follow this system you will enjoy the financial rewards of a growth company.

If I have not scared you away yet and you do decide to start on this journey, then my advice is do not compare yourself to anybody other than the best.

Never satisfy yourself by saying, *"It has been a quiet month, but it's ok because everybody else is quiet", or "The summer is always quiet", or "My friend's uncle's business had a quiet month last quarter."*

Don't satisfy yourself by comparing against anybody other than the very, very best. Only by being the very, very best, will you stand any chance whatsoever of successfully staying in business and producing the good financial returns that you will need and deserve.

Learn from the Past, but Don't Dwell on It

Whilst it is useful to study your trading history, by the time you read the Profit & Loss accounts, there is nothing you can do to affect them. A Profit & Loss account is a statement of history not a projection of the future. Some business leaders become obsessed with the historical financial ratios of their past trading, just as some people become obsessed with all the things that went wrong in their childhoods. To be successful, as a person and as a business owner, you should spend more time looking forwards than backwards. That's not to say that you can't look at your past trading. Learn from the past so you can assess how it impacts your sales today and tomorrow but don't spend too much time on it.

The only two trading periods that matter are today's and tomorrows. Not yesterday, or last week or that record-breaking quarter three years ago. You cannot do anything about yesterday, so in order to move forward you need to look forward.

Climbing a Mountain – Every. Single. Day.

Wake up every morning at 6.00am, have a good breakfast, arrive at work by 7.00am, get the team together, align yourself to your vison and set out a plan to have the best possible day leading your team. I often describe business leaders as mountaineers because the task of leading a business can feel like an uphill climb. Like a mountaineer, a business leader needs to have a clear plan, inspire the team, lead from the front, share knowledge and expertise, highlight risks and constantly push on to drive the whole team higher and higher.

Now, climbing a mountain seems like a difficult task, but the challenge of climbing a mountain will fade into insignificance when compared against the task of building and running your own successful business. It is going to feel like climbing a mountain every day. Not only some days, but every day. You will climb a mountain on Monday, followed by climbing a mountain on Tuesday, Wednesday, Thursday and Friday. Unfortunately, it will also feel like climbing a mountain on Saturday and Sunday before climbing the next mountain on Monday. Have no doubt, if you wish to run a successful business, prepare yourself for lots of relentless mountain climbing. But when you reach the top of each mountain the view can be glorious and worth the climb.

A Head Above the Rest

Look for the opportunity to raise the standard. Find as many different ways as you can to lift the bar above your competitors. If they are offering 'next week' delivery, offer 'this week' delivery. If they are offering 'this week' delivery, offer 'delivery tomorrow'. If they are offering 'delivery tomorrow', offer 'delivery today'. And if they are offering 'delivery today', offer delivery before they even know they want your product or service.

Make sure your unique selling point really is unique. Many businesses consider that their USP is a wonderful level of service. They believe that their product/service is better than all the competition. But for most business owners that is just their opinion – it is a claim based on what they believe as opposed to testing against the market and having a real understanding of where their service ranks in the mind of their customers, or how it benchmarks against their competition. So, make sure when you are describing the unique selling point of your product or service, there really, really is a unique aspect to it – something that no one else is offering.

When businesses have been trading for a number of years, it is very easy for the leaders to lose sight of how their competitors have upgraded their service offer. The opportunities to use technology, design and creativity to enhance the quality of service has grown dramatically. Logistics management has transformed many business models and it is creating shock waves throughout many sectors. It is easy to become blindsided by the service improvements of competitors, so it is important to constantly benchmark your offer against those of your competitors. The higher your standards, the more difficult it will be for competitors to steal your customers. The higher your standards, the more difficult it will be for competitors to enter your market. The higher your standards, the better gross and net margins you will earn from customers.

Complacency kills businesses. Past glories, awards, trophies and letters from customers thanking you are all designed to lull you into a false sense of security. Last year's great profits make your sun lounger look so attractive. The best quarter deserves a round of golf. A new customer deserves a Friday afternoon off. However, if you want your business to be successful and if you want your growth to accelerate beyond that of your competition, then the prescription is easy: never rest whilst the competition work. Never take joy in yesterday's successes. Never sleep comfortable in your bed or become complacent because of the big order you have just won. Never take comfort in having the best sales today or the best sales last week. Today's successes can and will disappear, before you know what has happened, they can become just a sweet memory. Like sand banks that move relentlessly with each daily tide, business success can quickly come undone. The world is littered with businesses that were once great and now have the CLOSED sign permanently affixed on the front door.

You must never become comfortable or complacent. This does not mean that you should forget to celebrate your successes. This is critical. You must recognise achievement and your staff by wholeheartedly celebrating their achievements before you return to the next daily battle.

Financial Arrangements

It is critical to find an excellent accountant. They will ensure you are trading in the most appropriate way to: reduce risk, drive sustainable profits, raise finance, protect your assets, minimise tax and engage other stakeholders in a proper set of arrangements. An accountant will help you set up a financial plan to: drive income, control overheads, save time and money, look after the detail, keep you up to date on statutory matters, manage your payroll, produce cashflow budgets, draft Profit and Loss forecasts, complete monthly management accounts, set up daily reporting systems for sales/gross profit/Key Performance Indicators (KPIs), construct year end accounts and complete taxation calculation, which can be submitted to the government. The selection of your accountant, therefore, is significant. To find a good accountant ask other successful business owners to recommend one, review their websites, check them out with financial bodies, review the partners and staff to see if they have the specialisms you will require from your accountant. Interview several accountancy firms, to see if you can establish good effective communications with them, finally, review their fee structure to make sure it is fit for your purpose. As you grow, it is likely you will need to upgrade and change your accountant so that they can advise you at each stage of your growth.

With Growth Comes Change

When a business achieves an accelerated level of growth, it will undergo significant change in all areas. This includes marketing, IT, manufacturing, finance, operations, innovation, HR, quality and sales. It is inevitable that the roles will grow. The scale, complexity and risk associated with each senior role will grow every time the company grows and the requirements of your teams in these areas grow. I have diagrammed this growth in Figure 1. If you look at the graph, you can see the relationship between growth of the team responsibilities and the impact this has on the scope of the individual's role. As the business grows the scope of the job and what is needed to succeed, is impacted. This constant company growth will test the ability of the original staff and many of your teams will grow and thrive from this opportunity for growth. However, not everyone will be able to keep up and this is where you must offer training and development to support them so that their growth coincides with the company's growth

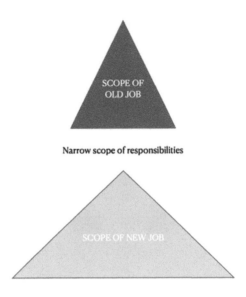

Fig. 1: Accelerated Growth

If after offering support, team members are unable to make a solid and comparable contribution to the vision of the company, then the leaders must not falter from having difficult discussions; either to offer more support to those struggling, or to encourage them to find other opportunities better suited to them. These conversations are never easy, but the stress that can be caused by requiring a member of staff to perform at a level they cannot meet can result in destructive consequences. It is irresponsible to leave a struggling member of staff in a role where they cannot perform. The fairest option is to support them with training and mentoring, if there is no improvement, move them onto alternative opportunities within or outside the company. This dashboard can be used to track the performance of the team against the KPIs for productivity and growth capability.

STAFF INDICATORS

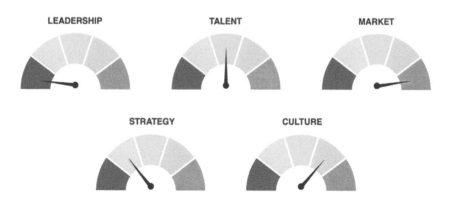

Inspiration Comes from the Top

Do not 'manage' your team, 'inspire' them. Many managers and leaders I talk to tell me about how they 'manage' their teams but when I look at their businesses and their staff, they are more reminiscent of a morgue. Corpses everywhere. A morgue is full of dead people, no energy, no hope, no joy, no passion and no long-term goal. A business run like a morgue will never set a customer on fire. Customers need to feel the passion and energy of your staff. To ensure your staff demonstrate passion, energy and drive when dealing with your customers, you need to inspire them every day. 'Managing' staff is never going to be good enough to accelerate your growth, you must 'inspire' your teams and align them to the high growth targets you have set for yourself.

You can get at least 10%, 20%, 30% or 40% more from your staff when you inspire them and give them the chance to do their absolute best. Inspire your staff, lift them up, fill them with energy, share your vision and excite them. Make them jubilant about sharing your mission and helping you to deliver your product and service in an exceptional fashion to your customers. Inspiring your team costs nothing, but the return on investment will be huge. Demonstrate in your behaviours that you trust your staff, believe in them and their abilities. Give them your attention, get to know them, understand what drives them and engage them in your vision.

From the top down, all leaders and team members need to be driven, passionate and convey a sense of urgency. This should come from the understanding that all businesses operate in a world that casts an appropriate sense of peril over all companies. The sense of peril is driven by the ceaseless demands of customers to improve, the remorseless pressure from competitors trying to steal your market share, the changing landscape of legislation and H&S requirements and the need to balance financial arrangements. But this is not something to fear - it is this sense of peril that ensures relentless drive and energy. This sense of peril is your best friend. There is no need to be constantly stressed – just an awareness of the peril in the business world can motivate you to lift your standards and provide the drive to pursue your goals every day.

Don't Lose Your Momentum

If you want to achieve anything, you have to build up energy. Like the old steam trains, you have to light a big fire under the boiler and build up a huge head of steam. It's not sufficient to put just a little bit of energy behind your business. If you want to really achieve something, go faster than the rest and climb the highest mountains, then you are going to have to build a ton of momentum.

Building up a head of steam with your staff can take a considerable amount of time, but once you have built it, guard it with your life. If you build up momentum with your staff and they are dancing with you to the tune of your vision, you must never let the pressure drop. If you do loose the momentum, if the steam does leak, rebuilding a head of steam will be really, really tough. Unlike the grand old Duke of York, you can march them up to the top of the hill once, but if they come back down, you will really struggle to march them back up again. So, once you have built up that head of steam, energy, passion and enthusiasm, do not let it drain away. If you ease off or if you become complacent, you lose the energy, then you lose the momentum that you have generated.

Remember there is only one first prize. There is only one Apple, one Ferrari, one Chanel, one person who breaks the four-minute mile and one person to be the first to step foot on the moon. Be that company. Be that leader. Make sure you win the first prize.

10 Golden Tips

1. Do not compare yourself against any other business or leader than the best.
2. The only two trading periods that matter are this one and tomorrow's - not yesterday's.
3. Climb a steep mountain every day.
4. Look for the opportunity to raise the standard.
5. Make sure your Unique Selling Point is 'Unique'.
6. Appoint an excellent accountant.
7. Never rest, drive towards your goal every day.
8. Do not manage your team, inspire them.
9. Build up a head of steam and keep the momentum at all cost.
10. There is only one first prize.

KEY LEARNINGS

CHAPTER 1

1.

2.

3.

ACTION PLAN

CHAPTER 1

ACTION	WHO	PRIORITY	STATUS	NOTES	DUE DATE
1.					
2.					
3.					
4.					
5.					
6.					

2

WHY?

· · · · · · · ·

Before you can give customers a great product or service, you have to understand why you want to do this. Is it because you want to be the hand protection specialist of the world? Is it because you want to deliver great diamond tipped drills for craftsmen? Is it because you want to bring the best marble or the best tiles from around the world into the UK to give people wonderful homes which they can relax in and enjoy their time with their families?

Once you have understood your 'Why', you can really start to drive and deliver on your vision. If you have a really strong 'Why', it will sustain and motivate you during the tough long days ahead. The stronger your 'Why' the easier it is for your staff to follow and drive your business forward. If your 'Why' is clear and strong, customers will be able to better understand what you stand for and what they can expect when they engage with your business.

In 2009 Simon Sinek wrote a book called "Start with Why" which promoted the importance of business leaders understanding their Why. The book started a movement to inspire people at work and in turn inspire customers.

We need a plan

If you do not know where you are going, how will you ever know when you have arrived? You would never set out on a long car journey to a new destination without a map or satellite navigation system to guide you, so don't be tempted to run your business without a plan. This plan will form part of your business plan. It is near impossible to establish a successful business without a clear, succinct plan. This does not have to run to 700 pages, full of endless detail which no one will ever read. It can be a simple one-page plan, or it can be a 15-page plan, whatever suits your purpose. What is important, is that it sets out a beginning, a middle and crucially, an end point – an end point so that you know when you have arrived. Your plan needs distinct numerical targets, clear ownership and deadlines. This will guide you and your team to stay on track and take the corrective action when necessary to arrive at your chosen destination.

Find Support Before You Need It

Remember, you can't do this on your own. You have to be the spark; you have to bring the life to the plan. You have to have the vision. You have to start the energy. But you cannot do this on your own, you need to find support from a number of different sources. Think of it like recruiting your very own Fan Club. First of all, you need family support, which should be established before you start the business. Many hours will be worked during family time, weekends and holidays. Communicate with them, share your vision, make sure you are on the same page as them so that they support your endeavor. It is difficult enough starting and running a successful business, so you need to build up your emotional bank account with your family.

You need your friends. They can help to bounce ideas around, bring talents to your new business and broaden your networks for resources, support and sales.

Last but not least, you need your staff. It may come as a shock when you first discover that just paying staff a wage or salary will not necessarily translate into securing their support. Staff need a financial deal to work in your business, but to bring their souls, passion and energy to the business, they need to be inspired by you and inspired by your vision for the business. So, you need to make sure you clearly communicate what you are going to try and do.

Engage as many people as possible because you will be surprised how many times you will need those friends, family and staff along the way. Make a few very strong promises to yourself before you start, remember what is important and who is important and don't lose sight of this when building your business. You can very easily get sucked into the vortex of making your business successful and sustainable and loose perspective.

Think Hard About Your Customers and Staff

Live in your customers shoes. Put them on and walk around in them for a couple of days. Do not settle into the satisfaction of your comfy armchair and say to yourself, "Yes, I think we are all doing very well". Be critical of yourself. Be tough on yourself. Ask yourself, "Am I really delivering to my customers the vision of products and services I promised myself when I started this business?". The best business leaders I have worked with are never happy with the status quo. No matter how much they improve on one day, they wake up the next driving for a big improvement; a step change in service or an innovation to a product. This restless and constant search for improvements ensures that you stay ahead of your competition.

In order to get the best staff in the world, you need to be deserving of the best. Treat them kindly and with respect. Hold them accountable. Offer them challenges and be sure to give them opportunities to stretch themselves. Your staff are your team so train and develop them. No sports manager worth their salt would ever play anything but their best team, so make sure your business team are the very best. It is easy to compensate for the poor performance of one of your team or to turn a blind eye and look the other way, but this will never be a long-term solution. 'See it, Say it, Sort It' - if at some point you should look over your shoulder and see that you have lost a good member of staff, or you have lost the support or commitment from your staff, this is the time to pause, turn around, go back and understand why. Do not shrug away from having that challenging discussion with your staff to figure out why they are no longer aligned to the agenda. Do not make up your mind about them without giving them the opportunity to get back on board or for you to learn. If they remain out of sync and do not take up the opportunity for further training and support, have a handshake and accept it is time to say goodbye. Not all members of your team will withstand your business journey and that is ok.

Customer Excellence

One of the key drivers for business leaders is the desire to provide excellent customer service. Over the last ten years it has become harder and harder to demonstrate that your customer service is cutting edge. Many larger companies are now deploying technology to exceed customer expectations for same day delivery, tracking information and frictionless sales. So good service standards from ten years ago can now look dated only because the competition has caught up and moved beyond this standard. The iceberg graph below highlights that when we are trying to understand what we need to do to improve customer service the answers can be found by listening to the customer. Although business leaders will have a view, managers will have data and front line will have their side of the story, it is only by listening to the needs and experience of the customers that leaders can hope to find the gold dust. If business leaders want to find ways to improve customer service, then they should listen to their customers.

It's All About Balance

Work/life balance is not a choice. If you make it a choice, you will never get a work/life balance. You must make sure you balance out time, work and energy, ensuring that there is enough time for you and the ones you love. Check yourself regularly and if you have lost the work life balance that suits you and your family – fix it. You are never going to work this hard in any other occupation. Doctors, nurses, dentists, teachers, politicians, biscuit makers, car makers, exhaust repairers, they all work really hard. They all work hard in their own way. But nothing will ever feel as challenging as running your own business. It's not just the hours, it's the mental agility required, it is the constant

ICEBERG

WHO KNOWS THE MOST ABOUT OUR BAD SERVICE PROBLEMS

Your knowledge of the problem

Your managers knowledge of the problem

Your frontline staff knowledge of the problem

Your customers knowledge of the problem

need to make the point responsibly, to take people with you, to build up a head of steam. Buy yourself a good diary and have a valuable session with it on a regular basis. Book in the important times with family and friends. If you secured their support at the launch of the business, they will have made lots of contributions and sacrifices for you along the way. Therefore, make sure you plan the times when you give back to this fan club. Their ongoing support is not guaranteed so you need to constantly reinvest your time and passions back to them if you want long-term membership.

Play to Win

You can win big in business, but you can easily lose big too. As your business starts to grow, you will end up putting more and more of your eggs in one basket. Carry that basket really carefully, you can't afford to smash the eggs because they never go back together very well (ask Humpty Dumpty).

If you are going to play this game, make sure you play to win. Understand and be honest with yourself about where the finishing line is. If you do not know where the finishing line is, how will you ever know when you have won the race? If your objective is to turn over a million pounds, or £10 million, or £20 million, or £30 million, write it down. If you want to be the first billionaire in your city, your town, your street or your house, place that marker as your finishing line. That finish line will determine when you have won the race and when you can take comfort in your success.

Once you have crossed the finishing line, the planning for the next race begins and you start the cycle all over again - but this time informed by what you learned in the previous race. Do not just finish a race and start the next one without a good review. Learn from the journey. Allow yourself to celebrate but then stop, breathe deeply, reflect, learn, build your learnings into your new plan and renew the spirit before the next race starts. Friends and family are those who will help you achieve it, so share the celebrations with them too.

10 Golden Tips

1. Before you can give customers a great product or service, you have to understand Why you want to do this for customers.
2. If you do not know where you are going, how will you ever know when you get there?
3. You cannot do this on your own, you will need family, friends and staff to support you.
4. Make a few very strong promises to yourself before you start and hold yourself to them.
5. Live a day in your customer's shoes.
6. You deserve the best staff in the world.
7. Work/life balance is not a choice.
8. You will never work this hard in any other occupation.
9. You can win big and lose big, so play to win.
10. Understand and be honest with yourself about where your finishing line is.

KEY LEARNINGS

CHAPTER 2

1.

2.

3.

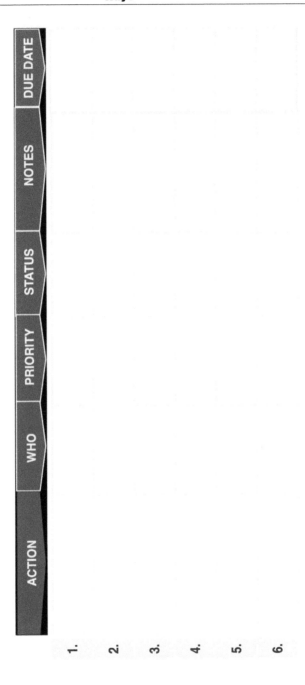

ACTION PLAN
CHAPTER 2

ACTION	WHO	PRIORITY	STATUS	NOTES	DUE DATE
1.					
2.					
3.					
4.					
5.					
6.					

3

DEFEND THE CORE BUSINESS

· · · · · · · · · · · · ·

There are lots of ways to grow a business and many strategies are good common sense. In this chapter and the three that follow, I will present my system for growth within a four-stage framework. Some business owners hope their businesses will grow. Some business owners spend their lives looking for silver bullets to drive their business growth. Some businesses owners listen to stories of business greatness in bars, golf clubs, PTA meetings and the gym. I offer none of these solutions in this book. I strongly recommend following this system for accelerating the growth and sustainable profits of your business. This system is set out in chapters three, four, five, six and seven.

- **Defend the Core Business**
- **Develop into Adjacent Markets**
- **Big Hairy Audacious Goals**
- **Consolidate your Growth**

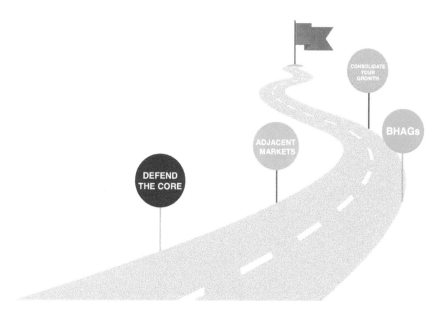

Define Your Business

Before you can grow a business, you have to be able to define it. You need to be able to map out everything you know about your existing business so that you are aware of the limit of its resources, talents, customer base, USPs, finances and supply chains. This is really important because before you can grow your business, you need an honest appraisal of what your business looks like now.

Once you are able to map out the core of your existing business, you will gain a deep understanding of what you need to do to defend it.

As you can see in Fig. 2, I have broken this case study into three main areas, which are essential when it comes to understanding the business's capacity for growth;

1. Products or Services
2. Staff
3. Customer Base

Each of these three areas are critical. Anything short of excellence on the part of your products/services, staff and customers will affect your capacity for growth. We will talk more about this in a bit, but for right now, let's talk generally about defending your core.

Fig. 2 is an example of how I try to conceptualise the shape of a company. As you know, all businesses have unique features; some have strong physical assets, some have a strong product innovation, some will have highly skilled staff and others may have a wide or a narrow geographical focus. Fig. 2 shows the shape of an imaginary company based around foundational aspects.

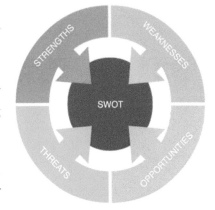

Once you are able to conceptually map out the core of your existing business, you will gain a deep understanding of what you need to do to defend it. Please note, I am not expecting you to actually draw

Fig.2 Defend the Core

This is an example company.

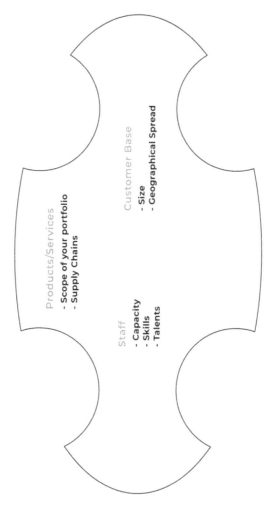

Products/Services
- Scope of your portfolio
- Supply Chains

Customer Base
- Size
- Geographical Spread

Staff
- Capacity
- Skills
- Talents

The above conceptual shape is fictitious but demonstrates that all companies have different strengths and weaknesses making their form unique.

the shape of your business on paper, when I say 'draw' or 'map', I am encouraging you to write a list of all the aspects of your company so that you are aware of your strengths, weakness, opportunities and threats (SWOT).

Take some time to map out the core of your business by undertaking a SWOT (using Fig. 2 as a guide). Review your balance sheet, gather customer feedback and looking closely at your product range and service delivery. Each part of this review will help you understand the health of your core business as it stands today. Get specific here and include as many details as possible (so long as they pertain to the core business). Write down critical information from your sales and marketing efforts, including:

- Your sales trend over the last three years (is it increasing, flattening out or decreasing)
- Your level of margins generated from sales as a trend over the last three years (increasing, flattening out, decreasing)
- The strength of your balance sheet
- Your e-commerce and social media capacity

In Fig.2 You will also notice pockets and indentations around the outside of the core business. They represent areas of potential growth - areas for adjacent market development. We will look at them in the next chapter.

Defend the Core Business

The conceptual outline in Fig. 2 is the framework that we shall describe as your core business. This is the basis of your future growth. This is your foundation and the goose that lays the golden eggs. Whatever action plan you develop or decisions you make about your future growth, they must not damage the core business or kill the goose.

The very first thing you do when you get into work is to defend the core business. The core business is your enduring asset. It is the part that pays the bills and puts the money in the kitty for the next stage of development. You have to do everything possible to defend this core and avoid anything that will damage it. There will be lots of exciting temptations, new distant markets, big corporations, R&D projects and yes, the grass will always look greener on the other side, but defending the core must come first.

How do you go about defending your core business? The answer is in the details. They may seem insignificant on a minute-to-minute basis, but collectively, they protect the core. Below is an example of a checklist you can use to review your core business.

Protect the Core Checklist	Check
• You have got to offer great service	
• Answer the phone with a smile	
• Make sure your Unique Selling Points (USPs) are unique and not tired	
• Check that you deliver on the promises you make	
• Ensure your logistics are perfect (every day)	
• Plan for the future and keep this plan alive	

• Get the right pricing policy	
• Control your finances and never forget how you make money	
• Inspire your team with huge amounts of energy and lead with humility	
• Listen carefully to customer feedback and act upon it to enhance your value proposition	
• Constantly look for innovations to improve your products and services	
• Nurture the creativity of your staff and keep energy levels high at all times	
• Invest in staff training to capacity build the whole team	
• Keep your premises looking and functioning smartly	
• Build smart technology into all aspects of your customer interactions	
• Get ahead of environmental and sustainability issues	
• Be seen to deliver 100% quality	
• Enhance the value of your brand	
• Get close to all your customers to secure their ongoing business and identify new needs	

Above is a checklist, make sure you do all of these things. As well as this there will be another long list of actions which are specific to your business. Make a list of the details that reflect your business' unique situation and follow through on them. This is defending your core business. Geese that lay golden eggs have a nasty habit of dying if they feel neglected and unloved. They sense a lack of commitment and give up.

I have visited a business in distress with the business owners clueless as to why their business was not growing. One short visit to the business car park revealed, tiles missing from the front doorstep, weeds in the gutters, paint peeling from the facia and litter strewn across the car park. These items of untidiness where not necessarily the problem, but they were indicative of the lack of attention which was being given to the business. Within one day the exterior of the business was improved, which was significant only because it signaled a turning point. It sent a message to the staff, customers and suppliers that this business is being loved and given attention. The company went on to grow as each part of the organisation was brought back to life and produce significant growth in profits.

Make sure you know who and what your best assets and talents are. Make sure they are polished and on display where everyone can see them. Shine a light on them. Tell people about them. Shout about them. Use social media, your website, your staff and your sales literature. Everybody should know the best talents and assets that you have in the business.

Case studies, endorsements and recommendations from named people can have real value. Get clarity quickly about what you need to adjust to defend the core of your business. Is it your environmental standards? Is it your customer service? Is it your premises? Your location? Your menu? Is it your staff uniforms? What is it that makes your business so valuable that it can lay golden eggs? Once you know make sure you do it, day in, day out. This sounds so obvious, but you would be amazed how many businesses spend too much time chasing dreams of big new projects which will bring huge new sales and consequently let their core business suffer. Do not let this happen to you.

When you are trying to generate new ideas for your business you do not have to sit under a tree hoping the apple will fall onto your head. The best way to systemise the development of new ideas for your business is to listen to key stakeholders who will have golden insights to share with you. Make sure you put time aside to ask open questions to; your staff, suppliers, customers, competitors, review the market and bring all of this feedback together in a SWOT. (as set out in the diagram below)

PROCESS TO GENERATE NEW IDEAS FOR PRODUCTS OR SERVICES

CASE STUDY

Smith Tile Imports Ltd is a company that imports and resells flooring tiles. This company has had static sales for the last three years with slipping margins and a shrinking customer base. Competitors are taking many of their customers and good staff have been leaving for jobs at companies who are new to the market. Supply lines are drying up, cash is running short and marketing has resorted to promotions, discounts and special offers.

In understanding their short falls and problems, an action plan can be drawn up to defend their core. The defend the core plan must address basic foundational issues. It does not have to be clever, but it does have to strengthen the basics. Once we have the foundations strengthened, we can build upwards. But if we try to resolve foundational issues with a lick of paint, we are deluding ourselves. This is the time to roll up your sleeves and get to the root of the rot. Judging from their situation, the action plan I would draw up for them would look something like this:

- Get out to customers and investigate their current needs and pain points
- Restate the vison for your company
- Secure new talent for sales and marketing
- Inspire the whole staff team, engaging them to drive the renewed company vision
- Engage the supply chain to reinvigorate the product portfolio
- Invest in online sales

- Train and qualify all staff with high class customer service skills
- Restate your customer service levels for quoting, delivery and service
- Boost reselling, cross selling, conversion rates and business development
- Drive referrals from existing customers
- Focus on growing the pipeline
- Push debtor days, agree finance options and reduce unnecessary overheads

If their 'defend the core' plan is followed every day by the whole company, the business will become stronger, financially secure and sustainable.

Many people mistakenly assume that a company like Smith Tile Imports is doomed – that they have had their time to shine and now other competitors are taking their turn. But this is not the case. Before giving up on a company, work through the actions outlined in the Defend the Core Checklist on the previous page, take the time to define its core and do everything you can to defend that core. Time and time again companies have shown incredible comebacks. Believing it is possible and doing the work to define and defend the core is critical to success. Sticking your head in the sand will not resolve any of the issues listed. Sometimes businesses are lost because the owner convinces themselves that it is not their fault they are losing money and the solution is out of their control. I have listened to many business owners describe the poor weather, the political environment, the economic cycle or online stores undercutting their prices. Sadly, in many cases this is delusional. Most business problems are self-inflicted due to poor leadership over several years and this is why it is critical for business owners to pay attention every day to defending the core and renewing the relevance of their business to current market conditions.

Deliver on Your Promises

Many businesses will boast that they deliver truly exceptional service. It is so easy to say: "We deliver exceptional service!" and this is often proclaimed on their websites. But do they really deliver exceptional service? Do you? Do you go beyond the extra mile? How does your service compare against the best in the market? Do you do the hard yards? Do you push yourself? Do you do extraordinary things for customers (when no one is looking)? Or do you just deliver a mundane, average level of service for your customers? Maybe your service was exceptional two years ago, but since then your competitors are offering free, same day two-hour delivery. Maybe turning a quote round in 24 hours was exceptional a year ago, but now customers expect instant quote turnarounds. Is your customer service 'wow' or 'thick, gloopy and going nowhere'? I am always bemused when a customer decides they have a need for your service, digs out your contact details, reaches out to you, asks you for a price to buy something from you and the business says - "we will send our quote through next week". This invites the customer to call your competition to request a quote from them. More often than we like to admit it, the order will go to whoever comes back quickest with the quote. The argument I hear is that "we are special, our product is bespoke, it just takes a few days to work out a quote." I doubt this is reality. I have seen businesses improve their quote cycle from 10 days to 18 seconds. It was no surprise this company went on to experience a strong growth in sales. The lengthy quoting timescale was a product of tradition and overload due to an overly bureaucratic old manual system which delivered a perfect quote to the penny. The customer however had an updated requirement for immediate quotes. Customer needs had changed and the business had not noticed. Initially the quoting team could not be persuaded that this need for an immediate quote could be met. However, once the quoting team could see the impact it had on their conversion rates and better understood the needs of their customers, they were able to innovate a new solution which met the customers needs.

Stand back and put on your customer's shoes. Look at the service level and ask yourself, "Is it truly exceptional?". The best way of testing whether or not your business is delivering exceptional service is to keep close to your customers. No matter how big you get, no matter how professional you get, or how celebrated you become, make sure you spend sufficient time listening to customers. Do not use this as an opportunity to tell them how great you are but listen and test your model against their expectations. One chairman of a £500m company that I know, still rings ten customers a day, randomly selected, to check their feedback on how his business is providing them with the service they need. This commitment to constantly collecting customer feedback means he is able to validate if his customers are experiencing the high levels of service required to keep them loyal. This is easy for any business owner to do - just pull the names and contact details of 10 customers off your sales ledger each day call them to ask if you have delivered on your promise of exceptional customer service.

Another great way to find out if you are delivering great customer service is to use mystery shopping. Ask family, friends or other business owners to test your systems by calling and making enquiries, using your website and buying goods to validate your claims for packaging and delivery processes. Set this up by fully briefing the mystery shopper about what you hope they will discover and then give them a scenario to test the customer service promise. Make sure staff are given all feedback whether it is good or whether it highlights areas for development.

Keep Your Standards Sky-High

Lead from the front. You cannot sit back in the office and tell your frontline sales staff to go out and make it happen. You have to be able to get out there, stand amongst them, show them how it is done, lead from the front and manage the difficult tasks. Don't duck the awkward customer. Do not duck the complaints. Grab hold of the complaint. Get in touch with the upset customer. Get in front of the disappointed customer. Find out how you let them down. Find out where you could have done better.

Never let your standards slip. As soon as your standards slip it becomes a vicious circle. You unconsciously convey to your staff that this lower standard is okay, they then let the standards slip further. After six months of letting standards slip, even you will not recognise how much you have lost. Remember, your managers, staff and suppliers will never reach higher than the standards that you set for them.

Stick to the Knitting

Stick strictly to your own markets, sticking to the knitting and doing what you are good at. Do not start making furry giraffes in Outer

Mongolia. Somebody in the networking club may well have told you that it is the best thing they ever did. A parent at the school gate may have told you that this is how they made their fortune and it was simple, easy, quick and nobody ever gave them any competition it might sound exciting; it might sound different and crazy but do not believe a word of it. Stick to what you know. Only innovate within your known market. Stick to the knitting and do what you do but do it amazingly brilliant.

Before you move on to the next chapter, take the time to write out your action plan for defending the core business. Allocate all tasks to a named individual in the business and set up weekly reporting on all 'defend the core' KPIs. Set out the key areas of the business and list the key people in the business who will be taking responsibility to drive this defend the core improvement plan. Decide which actions you feel should be focused upon. The plan should be shared and reviewed each day at an early morning huddle with each of the key stakeholders. Based on performance determine the status of each area in respect of defending the core. In the simple example below, I have identified Customer Service and Operations as two areas which are Red and require significant urgent activity. Sales and Marketing are Amber and need to be addressed to protect the business. Finance is Green and is a strength. This is the hub of the core and the strength of the other areas needs to be built upon this strength.

Weekly report structure:

Owner	Defending the Core Business	Status
Julie – Customer Service	% calls dropped Quote within 10 minutes Customer Feedback 10 new customers onboarded Monthly	RED
Steve - Finance	Cash at bank Debtor days Gross Margin Breakeven Point Net Profit Free Cash	GREEN
Dana - Operations	OTIF Stock levels Old stock % Waste Same day deliveries Back Orders	RED
Bill - Sales	New customers Daily sales Follow ups Conversion rate Size of Sales Pipeline	AMBER
Edward - Marketing	Marketing Qualified Leads Retention Web Traffic Social engagement Business Development Pipeline Value	AMBER

This dashboard should be tailored to the company needs and monitored every day by the leadership team.

It may seem tedious to stop what you are doing and create a chart when you probably have most of this information in the back of your head. Having it down on paper, however, shows you what your business looks like now, so you know where your limitations are, what your resources are and where you are headed.

I have been amazed how many times struggling businesses have a senior team who believe the only route to future success lies in a new market opportunity. I have been able to use my system to arrest the decline of their existing business, grow their existing business and improve the profitability of their existing business. The growth, the profits are of course all good news, but this is only part of the story. The biggest win from this system is the confidence the business owner and senior team get from knowing how to run a company successfully. They can now take this confidence and use it to look for additional growth. I recently worked with a company who went through this part of the system and by simply defending the core business they enjoyed a 98% increase in sales within one year and were able to use the additional profitability to invest into adjacent markets.

Map out your core and work every single day to defend it.

10 Golden Tips

1. Define the core of your business in writing.
2. Promote your best talents and assets.
3. Get clarity about what you need to do to 'defend' your core business.
4. Deliver truly exceptional service.
5. Stay close to your customers.
6. Lead from the front.
7. Never ever let your standards slip.
8. Stick strictly to your known market.
9. Only innovate within your known market.
10. Stick to the knitting but do it amazingly brilliant.

KEY LEARNINGS

CHAPTER 3

1.

2.

3.

ACTION PLAN

CHAPTER 3

ACTION	WHO	PRIORITY	STATUS	NOTES	DUE DATE
1.					
2.					
3.					
4.					
5.					
6.					

4

DEVELOP
ADJACENT MARKETS

. . . .

Once you have the systems and processes in place to operate the business in a way to defend the core business seven days a week you can take the next step forward to accelerate the growth of your business. By defending the core, you will be enjoying increased gross profit, reduced overheads, increased productivity, increased sales, better customer retention, higher levels of conversion rates and higher levels of sustained profits and return on capital employed. You need to be able to evidence that you have got the core of the business settled and running like clockwork. You will need all your Key Performance Indicators (KPIs) in place and make sure they are consistently green. You need to develop an action plan to "defend the core business" with input from all your staff. Make sure you are doing all the things that you need to do to protect the goose that is laying the golden eggs – only at this point can you take the next step forward to accelerate the growth of your business.

A leader cannot micromanage all aspects of the business. So, it is vital that the leader establishes a small number of key performance indicators (KPIs) which the leader and the member of staff can use to direct their efforts. An example of KPIs may be;

- Sales
- Administration Errors
- Follow Ups
- One Time and In Full (OTIF)
- Quality Feedback
- Customer Service Rating
- Gross Profit Levels

KPIs should be set for the whole company. This process should start once the business plan has been agreed between the senior managers and the shareholders. Take the business plan and highlight all the activities (KPIs) which need to be executed if the whole plan is to be delivered. Then allocate every one of these activities (KPIs) to a member of the senior team, the senior team can cascade these activities (KPIs) down to their teams across the business - each person should have approximately 5 KPIs. A KPI should state what the required outcome is and the time scale to achieve it. It should be signed off with each member of staff and reviewed monthly through a 1:1 performance review with line managers. The senior team should then review the whole company KPIs once a month at the board meeting. This process ensures that the business plan drives all activity across the whole business and everybody's activity is aligned to the business plan via their line manager. This alignment and cascading of Business

Plan linked KPIs can have a dramatic impact on the ability of the organisation to execute the important issues which drive accelerated and sustainable growth.

Once you are confident that you have achieved the issues set out in chapter 3, your core business is clear and understood, you have established a system for defending your core business and it is operating consistently, you are ready to consider developing your business into the adjacent growth markets. Do not attempt this until you have proven that you have successfully defended the core business. An adjacent market can only be identified once you have mapped your existing market. (See Fig. 3.)

Map Your Customer Base

The starting point is to map your existing customer base. Who are you serving? Are they direct customers? Are they export markets? Are they business to business? Are they accessing your products via a distributor? Are they big businesses or small businesses? Are they using your product and making something else out of it? Do they buy your product or service online or via a retail/trade counter? Are you a component? Are you a subcontractor? Map out your existing customer base to clearly show who they are and what they spend money on (types of businesses, other products and services, etc.) These are the clues you need to gather and record so that you can identify your potential adjacent market opportunities.

Understand Your Expertise and Geographical Reach

The next thing to do is map your existing skills and competencies. Understand what you are good at and what your limitations are. Understand where you have expertise and where you need to grow. Understand what really makes your business different. Map your geographical reach - are you fantastic in the Northwest and Northeast but have no business in Scotland or the Highlands? Have you got great reach into Europe, but never served South America? Have you got a geographical reach in the six cities that are within 100 miles of your existing geographical location? By mapping your geographical reach, you know where your next steps should take you.

Adjacent Markets

Adjacent markets are an excellent way to grow your business whilst reserving cash and not increasing risk. An adjacent market is close to your core business. You can see in Fig.3 the example I have indicated that the adjacent markets are nuzzled up close to the core business. They should be in close proximity to your core business. Ideally, you are looking for opportunities to export your capabilities and skills into close next step markets. The adjacent markets are separate to your core business, but are still able to tap into existing networks, skills, competencies and capabilities. To find your adjacent market opportunities you must spend some of your time looking out of the windows of your business into the market to see where the close-by niches offer growth opportunities.

Fig. 3 Develop Adjacent Markets

This is an example company.

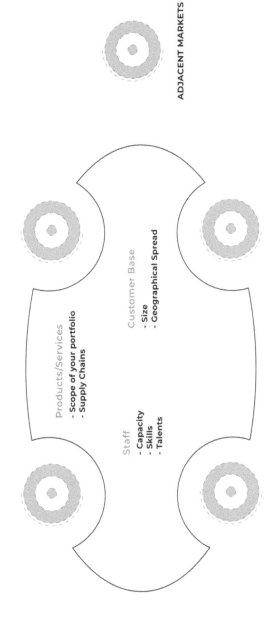

Products/Services
- **Scope of your portfolio**
- **Supply Chains**

Customer Base
- Size
- Geographical Spread

Staff
- **Capacity**
- **Skills**
- **Talents**

ADJACENT MARKETS

The above conceptual shape is fictitious but demonstrates that all companies have different strengths and weaknesses making their form unique.

Assess Your Risks

Map your existing supply base. Go and spend time with them and find out what they are making for your competitors. What are they planning on doing next year? What are the innovative products and services they are generating for two, three and four years out? Map your existing products or services and find out what people really use it for. Why do they buy your product over somebody else's? What is the added value in your product? If you are going to expand into one of the markets that you identify, you need to undertake a risk assessment. Two big rules apply, it is only an adjacent market opportunity if it can be developed with:

a) little or no additional risk
b) little or no additional capital.

If it does not pass this test then it is more likely to be a risky, capital hungry Big Hairy Audacious Goal (BHAG). If it is a BHAG, it is not a stage two adjacent market opportunity (we will look at these in more detail in the next chapter).

Risk Management

Many business leaders do not have risk mitigation high on their agendas. However, when I am asked to look at businesses who are struggling it is often because they have been blindsided to a risk which could have been foreseen and mitigated. Profit protection is rooted in the appropriate identification of risks and the resourcing of risk mitigation strategies which are reviewed regularly at board level. The diagram below gives you a visual tool for the mapping of your business risk.

Open Your Eyes to New Markets

In Fig. 3 you can see the original core business framework but built around the core business are areas that represent new market opportunities. These opportunities nuzzle up close to our core business – sometimes they are so close that we are blind to them.

Examples of adjacent markets might be:

1. Extending your product range by reducing plastic in an existing product
2. Extending your customer base via an additional passive export opportunity
3. Geographical expansion on a local basis
4. Increasing your operational capacity via same day delivery promise to gain new customers
5. Improve staff skills to enhance on-line sales

6. Extending sales reach by a customer portal roll out
7. Maximise your customer base by selling an existing customer a new product

The adjacent markets have to be close enough to your existing markets that you can still utilise your existing supply base. Sometimes because they are so close to your existing core business, they may have been discussed previously and discarded as unexciting you may have been blind to their potential. But now is the time to dust down all those previous ideas (large or small) and give them a new airing. Shine a bright light on these opportunities and find some hidden treasure very close to your core business.

Sometimes an opportunity for an adjacent market may be found in the waste from the manufacture of an existing product, such as turning coal dust into fuel briquettes. The opportunity can occasionally be found in the bi-product of a product or service, e.g. data, which can be much more valuable than the original product or service. The opportunity can be found by selling an additional product or service to an existing customer base, such as car finance along with the car sale. Maybe the product you are selling is a route to market for a service offer, like finance and loan services to people who buy clothes from catalogues. It may be airlines selling hotel slots or setting up wine clubs for their customers. Create some time in your agenda and gather you team around to explore potential adjacent markets. Undertake you review and feasibility study and produce a short list of ideas to take forward.

Innovation will be fundamental to your growth strategy. Some of the best innovations have come from the smallest of observations, the most incidental of customer feedback or the seemingly quietest of thoughts from the most junior member of your team. These observations in their simplest form are the gold dust of your accelerated growth and sustainability. Using the uncluttered input of a customer, an outsider or advisor can really enhance this process.

Adjacent Markets are Low Risk

You could expand geographically into the next region or locality. Some businesses are regionally based and technology now gives us an opportunity to sell online outside the confines of your traditional geographic boundaries. Many face-to-face services are now delivered via Zoom. Maybe your adjacent markets will revolve around product extension; you could develop your product to go from a Mars bar, to Mars bar ice cream, to Mars bar dark chocolate, to a Mars bar drink, to mini Mars bars, to big Mars bars and to Mars bar cookies. Do not stretch yourself too far. The power of developing into your adjacent markets is that it is a safe and low-risk way to develop your business. Do not overextend beyond the core business boundaries and do not push yourself too far from the core. Once you have decided what your adjacent market is and how you are going to do it, pilot test and prototype it before a big roll out and further investment. Track down feedback from customers, stakeholders and then bring the feedback back to base, review it and tweak your idea again before testing, piloting and prototyping again and again until you have a worthy new product or service to launch at low risk and low capital cost.

A company I have been working with recently used my system to identify an adjacent market opportunity close to their core business. This opportunity led them to secure a contract which drove an increase of 50% of their annual turnover within three weeks.

To further identify if you are looking in the right place for your adjacent markets you can use this process:

Adjacent Market Checklist	Y/N
Is it a market we can play in?	
Is it a market we can win in?	
Is it a strategy which has been developed around customer needs, wants, aspirations - fears concerns, apprehensions? (i.e. designed from the outside in?)	
Will it increase the number of transactions?	
Will it decrease our average transaction cost?	
Will it increase our transaction value?	
Is it aligned with our overall strategy?	
Will it increase enterprise value?	
Will it increase GP?	
Has it got minimal working capital absorption rate?	
Can we manage it within our existing risk minimisation system?	

10 Golden Tips

1. Map your existing market.
2. Map your existing customer base.
3. Understand what you are good at and what your limitations are.
4. Map your geographical reach.
5. Determine your existing supply base capability.
6. Map your existing product or service offer.
7. Use little or no additional risk or capital.
8. Identify new areas close to the existing core base for growth.
9. Do not overextend beyond the boundaries of your core business.
10. Pilot, test and prototype before rolling out.

KEY LEARNINGS

CHAPTER 4

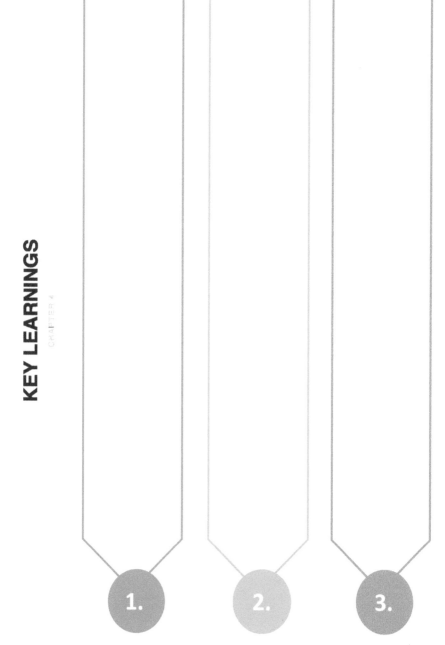

ACTION PLAN

CHAPTER 4

ACTION	WHO	PRIORITY	STATUS	NOTES	DUE DATE
1.					
2.					
3.					
4.					
5.					
6.					

5

BIG HAIRY
AUDACIOUS GOALS

• •

Before we shift to the next stage, let's recap to ensure you have got clarity. The system in chapter two helped you define your objective and developed a clear, driven plan backed by friends and family. In chapter three you defined the core of your business and examined how to go about defending that core (this is the job that must be completed before you attempt to grow your business, whether it takes one or ten years to defend the core.) In the last chapter, you considered developing into adjacent markets – developing into those areas close to your existing supply base, close to your geographical focus and close to your existing customers, through a small extension of your product or service. The development of the business into adjacent markets should produce an additional level of profit (over and above the planned profit from the core business). As a business leader you need to tread the correct path through the options of this system to reap the rewards. Defend the core, then develop into adjacent markets, then exploit big hairy audacious goals.

This additional level of profit can provide:

a) Additional shareholder returns
b) Project capital to invest in Big Hairy Audacious Goals (more on that soon).

For example, you can give half of the additional profit generated from the adjacent markets back to the shareholders for reinvestment in the core business. The other half of the additional profit can be utilised to pursue bigger, hairier, more audacious goals. These goals may well be focused around seeking new customers and insights beyond your current business boundaries, such as sourcing international or national inspiration for new products and services.

What is a BHAG?

BHAG is an acronym for Big Hairy Audacious Goal. BHAG was conceived by the American management guru Jim Collins. As an author in the field of sustainability and growth of companies, he used the term in 1994 for the first time in the ground-breaking book *Built to Last*, which he co-wrote with Jerry Porras.

BHAGs are ambitious long-term goals that can stimulate successful companies. Concrete, clear end goals are often what separate successful companies from less successful companies. It is precisely the pursuit of bold ideas that makes companies a head above the rest. A clear company goal within a certain time frame ensures a strong BHAG.

I created Fig.4 to help you visualize how these big hairy audacious goals are removed from the existing business markets. They are apart from the core business and not associated with the existing business model. Examples of BHAGs, besides mergers and acquisitions, would be:

- Co-design of new product with key customer
- Determined international expansion to significant markets
- Entry into diverse market in a significant fashion
- Radical restructure of manufacturing to utilise outsourcing
- Establish satellite business to test new idea

Identifying and Analysing Potential BHAGs

You may be able to identify big hairy audacious goals by inspecting your competitor base and looking at what opportunities they are pursuing. It

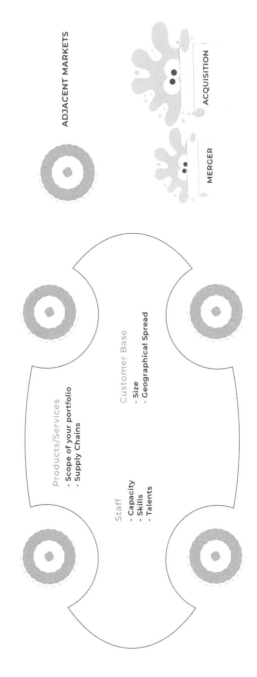

Fig.4 BHAGs

This is an example company.

ADJACENT MARKETS

ACQUISITION

MERGER

Products/Services
- Scope of your portfolio
- Supply Chains

Customer Base
- Size
- Geographical Spread

Staff
- Capacity
- Skills
- Talents

The above conceptual shape is fictitious but demonstrates that all companies have different strengths and weaknesses making their form unique.

may be an acquisition, a completely new range or a very different route to market. With the additional capital acquired by investing into the adjacent markets, you can expect to attract investment propositions, which will require thorough investigation and feasibility testing. Each potential BHAG idea will need to be filtered against a distinct set of criteria which will include:

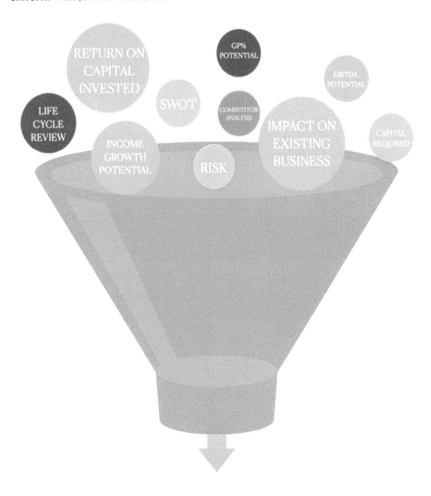

- Risk
- Capital required
- Return on capital invested
- SWOT (Strengths – Weaknesses – Opportunities – Threats)
- Competitor analysis
- Life cycle review
- Income growth potential
- GP % potential
- EBITDA potential (Earnings Before Interest Tax Depreciation and Amortization)
- Impact on existing business

Create a list for all potential BHAGs and then conduct a basic feasibility study to assess likely success, risk, capital required and return on investment in 12–60 months. This list can then be ranked and used to facilitate a selection process and a BHAG investment strategy.

Name a Champion Who Can Deliver

BHAGs are not guaranteed success and all investment projects should be viewed as high risk. They therefore require strong and consistent leadership. The individual you appoint must understand and be clear about the expectation on them to deliver on this exciting new project. The risk capital for this project has been generated from the development of the adjacent markets and so if it is a success, that is fantastic. If it is not a success, it is not the end of the world. You might have a bad day or even a week, but you will not end up having a bad 25 years because you have already banked the profits from the core business and reinvested 50% of the additional profits from the development of the adjacent markets back into your core business.

So, having identified where your next big hairy audacious goal might come from (after studying your customer base, your supplier base, your geographic base and your talents and skills) and having appointed a champion to lead it, now is the time for an exquisite state of planning and preparation.

Go or No Go: Don't Be Afraid to Walk Away

Having run your core business successfully and having developed a new pot of capital to fund these opportunities from adjacent markets, these big hairy audacious goals will demand and require significant planning and preparation. You cannot roll the dice on these riskier projects without taking due consideration. Agree clear 'go or no go' decisions at quarterly milestones so that you can walk away from a rotting, smelly big hairy audacious goals when required. Every three months agree an income or profitability target or an investment target. Review the distance travelled of the project and check on where the BHAG was expected to be by this date. Have a clear and challenging report of outputs on the development of the idea every three months. Review the report at your board meetings. Sit down and acknowledge that it was a great idea, you have put your hearts and souls into, and you have invested your capital into with good intentions. Recognise that you are now three months or six months or nine months on. You have to be honest with yourselves. If you are not making the progress that you wanted to make, challenge yourself to have a 'go, no go' decision at that point and be brave enough to walk away. There is no shame in walking away from a project that has failed, but there is shame in chucking good money after bad on a no hope 'ego' project. It is perhaps the hardest decision to walk away from a project which you have invested into and face the decision to write off the sunk costs.

However, there are two great quotes: "when you find yourself in hole – stop digging" and "do not throw good money after bad". This is why having clear milestones with pre agreed go and no-go decisions set out is so important.

Think Big (and Hairy)

Drive incredible energy and positivity into these big hairy audacious goals. If they are big, if they are hairy and if they are audacious, then they are going to need an incredible amount of energy to attain. Make sure that you can undertake a full post-mortem on all big hairy audacious goals. Win or fail, you need to understand why you had a certain outcome. You can use this learning to refine and improve the decision making and planning process next time you want to take out a big hairy audacious goal and invest the money that you have made from developing your adjacent markets.

In my own business we identified international markets as a BHAG. We undertook a deep desk review of 85 countries, country visits to 85 countries, feasibility studies on 27 countries and opening in 15 countries. I constantly defined the USP in each country based on market research into customer pain points and although the business in each country was based upon core values, there were distinct customer touch points which were unique to each market. These BHAGs stabilised the portfolio, raised the credibility in our home market, identified best practice which we were able to share across the group, boosted sales, compounded profits and positioned the company for further growth. The Gantt Chart below highlights the way key tasks need to choreographed to deliver a successful outcome.

10 Golden Tips

1. Do not progress further until your core business is secure and you have completed your growth in adjacent markets.
2. Use part of the additional capital created by developing the adjacent markets.
3. Seek new customer needs and insights beyond your current boundaries.
4. Seek international inspiration for new trends.
5. Inspect your competitor base for new developments.
6. Identify BHAG champions to lead and secure big results.
7. Require exquisite planning and preparation.
8. Agree clear go no-go decisions so that you can walk away from rotting BHAGs.
9. Drive incredible energy and positivity into your BHAGs.
10. Undertake full post-mortems on all BHAGs – win or fail.

KEY LEARNINGS

CHAPTER 5

ACTION PLAN

CHAPTER 8

ACTION	WHO	PRIORITY	STATUS	NOTES	DUE DATE
1.					
2.					
3.					
4.					
5.					
6.					

6

THE GROWTH CYCLE
· ·

L et's take stock of what we have already covered by using this system.

Stage One – Defend the Core

In chapter 3 you looked at defining and protecting the core business. The core business must be protected at all costs because this is the goose that is laying the golden eggs.

Stage Two – Develop Adjacent Markets

Only when the core business is safe and secure can you then move on to looking at stage two: mapping your potential adjacent markets. Remember, it is only an adjacent market when it utilises your existing customer

base, your existing products or services, your existing skill and talents, your existing supplier base and your existing geographical reach. Map all your existing assets. Identify business opportunities near to the core. Ensure limited amounts of capital and risks are expended. The outcome of stage two should be a pot of additional profits generated from this low risk activity.

Stage Three – Big Hairy Audacious Goals (BHAGs)

Once you have conquered stage two and driven profits from these adjacent markets, you can move to stage three. This stage is focused on identifying larger projects, capital hungry projects and riskier projects - commonly known as Big Hairy Audacious Goals (BHAGs). Attack big hairy audacious goals with tremendous vigour. They will be bigger, more capital intensive and riskier and will need close focus and leadership to be successful.

Stage Four - Consolidate

Once you have completed all the BHAGs, you need to evaluate them, learn from your successes and failures, bank the profits, lick your wounds and accept any losses. Only then can you move to stage four: the consolidation of all your activities.

Fig.5 Consolidating and Redefining the Core Business

This is an example company.

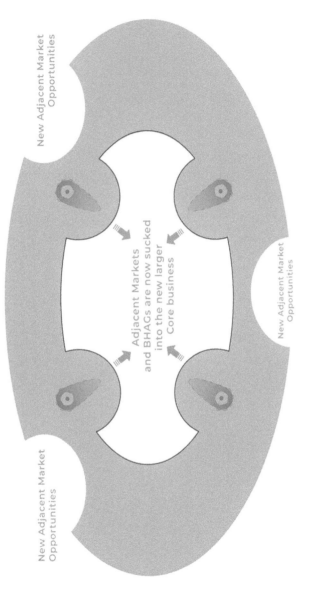

New Adjacent Market Opportunities

New Adjacent Market Opportunities

Adjacent Markets and BHAGs are now sucked into the new larger Core business

New Adjacent Market Opportunities

New Adjacent Market Opportunities

The above conceptual shape is fictitious but demonstrates that all companies have different strengths and weaknesses making their form unique.

Fig. 5 shows the core business sucking in all the adjacent markets and successful BHAGs inside a new expanded core business. The unsuccessful BHAGs can be discontinued, but only after you have fully diagnosed the project, recorded your learnings and filed all the data for possible future use. When all the successful BHAGs have been absorbed into the new core business, it will make the business a much larger, more diverse (new) core business, as shown by the expanding darker grey shape. This process of consolidation and redefinition should happen every three to five years. Those successful big hairy audacious goals that continue to have life should be pulled back into the center of the core business, so you redefine what the new core business is and start the growth cycle all over again.

Fig. 6 shows the growth cycle of defending the core business, expanding into adjacent markets, investing in BHAGs and finally consolidating the growth into your new core business.

Each time you reframe and renew the core business with your successful adjacent market developments and successful BHAGs, you strengthen the new core business through diversity, renewed lifecycles and investment. You will be widening your customer base and boosting your USPs for the benefit of new and existing customers. This growth and renewal of your core business will stretch the leadership, staff and systems in the business, but be aware and sensitive to these potential stretch marks – they will require support and long-term maintenance to enable them to keep up with the pace and rhythm of the business growth. I strongly support tactical training, development and mentoring of all leaders and staff in the business to cope and enjoy this growth journey. However, I do not support over stretching leaders and staff, as this can have dire consequences on mental health and work life balance, which is not a price worth paying. It is critical business

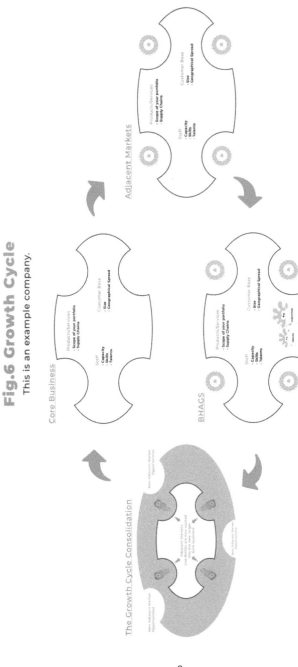

Fig.6 Growth Cycle
This is an example company.

The above conceptual shape is fictitious but demonstrates that all companies have different strengths and weaknesses making their form unique.

leaders ensure they and their businesses are always moving forward with high levels of agility. The diagram below sets out a framework for this winning mindset.

AGILE CORE VALUES
GROWING IN DYNAMIC TIMES

INDIVIDUAL AND TEAM
INTERACTIONS OVER
PROCESSES AND TOOLS

CUSTOMER
COLLABORATION OVER
CONTRACT NEGOTIATION

WORKING FLEXIBLY OVER
COMPREHENSIVE
DOCUMENTATION

RESPONDING TO
CHANGE OVER
FOLLOWING A PLAN

10 Golden Tips

1. Define and protect the core business.
2. Only when the core business is safe and secure should you move to the adjacent markets.
3. Map all your existing assets
4. Identify near-to-core business opportunities
5. Ensure limited amounts of capital and risk are expended.
6. When the adjacent markets have been conquered, you can move to the BHAGs.
7. Attack BHAGs with tremendous vigour.
8. Once complete, pull the adjacent markets and BHAGs into the centre and make it your new core business model.
9. Redefine your new core business.
10. Start the cycle again.

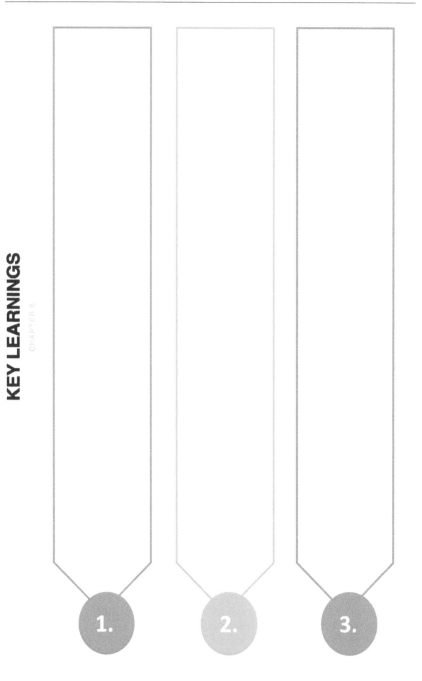

KEY LEARNINGS

CHAPTER 6

1.

2.

3.

ACTION PLAN

CHAPTER 6

ACTION	WHO	PRIORITY	STATUS	NOTES	DUE DATE
1.					
2.					
3.					
4.					
5.					
6.					

7

GROWTH CHARTING

. . . .

Lots of people I meet want company growth but do not have a plan. No plan = no growth, fact. Conversely, I have met some people who have a great big plan yet never achieve business growth in their lifetime. If you want to grow your business, I am asserting that you must have a certain type of plan. This plan must be written with the whole company's involvement; it must use simple language; use visual diagrams to promote engagement, understanding and excitement. The plan must be shared with all staff and kept alive to drive, enthuse and inspire growth.

Make a Plan and Break it Down into KPIs

Never start a growth trading period without a clear visual plan. Make sure all staff have contributed to the plan's development. Remember –

you can never hope to achieve an objective if you do not have everybody on board. This process of engaging all staff in the development of the plan will generate some great ideas and insights, but maybe more importantly, will secure cross company ownership of the plan and its required outcomes.

Once this visual plan is completed, give all staff a simplified visual copy. Make the visual plan accessible in the premises and refer to it in all meetings to guide day-to-day activity. The plan should be broken down into Key Performance Indicators (KPIs) with each element of the plan a separate KPI. Make sure each action in the growth plan becomes a KPI.

Each of the KPIs in the plan must be assigned to an individual member of staff. Leadership meetings, board meetings, head of department meetings and individual appraisals are driven using the KPIs. The performance of the business is underpinned by a bonus and incentive scheme to reward the achievement of the plan and additional stretch targets. KPIs are not a vehicle to beat up on staff, but an opportunity to properly agree and plan what needs to be done to achieve success. KPIs are an opportunity to engage and ensure that people who are in charge of important achievements have the resources they need, and the barriers removed, to give them the best chance of being successful. KPIs are a huge opportunity to celebrate effort, drive and success. KPIs are good and nothing to be scared of, they guide our efforts and highlight the desired outcome. The diagram below highlights the way a KPI Dashboard can provide focus and drive behaviours in key aspects of the company activity.

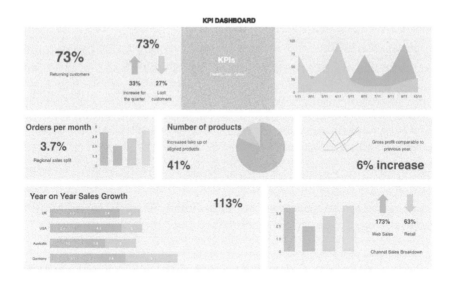

Incentives

I have designed many bonus and incentive schemes for my business over the years. My rule of thumb is that your business growth will accelerate if the staff are aligned to the financial growth of the business via salary, commission, incentives and bonus schemes. At the start of the financial year I agree a salary with all staff. The salary is paid on the basis of a job well done. Therefore, if somebody works all year and does an excellent job they are entitled to their salary. Some employers pay a salary and then if the employee does their job in an excellent fashion they pay them a bonus. I think this system sends the wrong message to the staff. You are paid a salary to do an excellent job. Sales staff will need a sense of drive to perform at the top level. Therefore, I would take the salary and pay 80% as a salary over 12 months. If the salesperson is achieving their sales targets, I would pay the salesperson the 20% of the commission back to them on a quarterly basis. By the end of the year the salesperson will have earned 80% salary plus 20% commission = 100% or their original salary. This allows the sales team to be part of the risk and reward scheme. Over performance can and should always be rewarded – win, win.

You may want to pay a salesperson a bonus for overachieving their sales target. In this example they would be paid 80% of their salary plus 20% commission plus a bonus payment for over achievement. In a none sales role a bonus could be paid for over performance e.g. finance team securing better payment days from customers, or in the logistics team maybe an improvement in the On Time and In Full (OTIF) target.

An incentive can be paid to drive a member of staff towards a unique goal i.e. open 10 new accounts per month or identify 3 new suppliers in our market. So, a member of staff could be paid a salary, commission a bonus and an incentive.

I recommend you consider setting targets for individuals which account for 80% of an incentive to be paid and the remaining 20% would be paid based on the achievement of the whole team. This ensures individuals are driven and the team comes together to enable everybody to secure full payment of the incentive.

I have used cross team targets to reduce the negative aspect of silos not working together for the good of the company. This would require each silo having to achieve cross team targets to earn their full incentive.

Finally, I would set targets for the whole year but make it clear to all staff that I intend to review and tweak all incentives, commissions and bonus's each quarter. This means that if the staff gamify their input to erroneously secure a payment you are able to tweak the criteria to ensure it stays on a win, win, win, basis. I would always honour the obligations to pay out at the end of each quarter, even if I could see the targets had been gamified. But I would tweak the scheme for the next quarter.

Salaries, incentives and bonuses can be paid to all staff whereas commissions are only paid to sales staff.

Your Growth Plan Needs to Be Seen

Plans and progress of plans should not be kept hidden in drawers, cupboards or on servers. A growth plan, if never seen, will never drive business growth. It is so easy to run out of petrol, overheat and break the speed limit in a car with no dials or dashboard. There is no point in having data available, progress reports, or KPIs if no one ever sees them. So, whether it is on computer screens, mouse mats, on the wall, in books or in the business plan, it does not matter just make sure it is seen. Make sure that the plan is a visual plan and it lives. Use colour, shapes and arrows to bring it alive. Fill the plan in during the course of the week, month or year to demonstrate if you are making progress towards achieving your priorities. Show progress towards the planned objective. Make it interesting by linking it to a recognisable design (think racing track, aircraft journey or mountain climb). This use of colour, form and fashion when reporting progress builds competition, a good sense of peril and a sense of achievement.

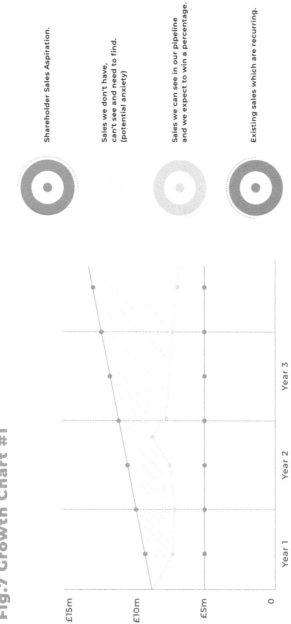

Fig.7 Growth Chart #1

Shareholder Sales Aspiration.

Sales we don't have,
can't see and need to find.
(potential anxiety)

Sales we can see in our pipeline
and we expect to win a percentage.

Existing sales which are recurring.

Fill Your Income Gap

Fig. 7 is an example of the way a plan may come together visually. The baseline shows the sales income the company has already secured, which is called the core business (see Fig. 2). The second line shows the percentage of income, which will hopefully be secured from the pipeline that you have been nurturing as part of your business development activity. By adding the baseline of existing business to the percentage of business you hope to win from your nurtured pipeline (including adjacent markets as shown in Fig. 3), you have a profile of your potential income over the next three years. However, the top line in Fig. 7 shows the shareholders expectation of required income. If that expectation is higher than the total of existing income, plus a percentage of your nurtured pipeline you have an income gap. This income gap needs to be filled with additional income that is not included from the first two segments. The worst situation is when leaders in the business 'hope' to fill up the income gap by just trying harder. This rarely (if ever) works. Instead it leads to bad decision making, stress, disappointment and financial losses. It is critical, therefore, when business growth planning to be able to specifically point to where the additional income is going to come from - this may include project management of BHAGs to fill the income gap. As you can see in Fig. 8, the income gap has been filled with BHAG projects (as set out in Fig. 4).

Get Focused on Your Three-Year Plan

So, what are the practical steps to take so that you emerge with a clear visual plan to drive your business growth? My answer: clear your mind to get focused on the next three-year trading period. There are going to be three distinct funding lines in your three-year plan:

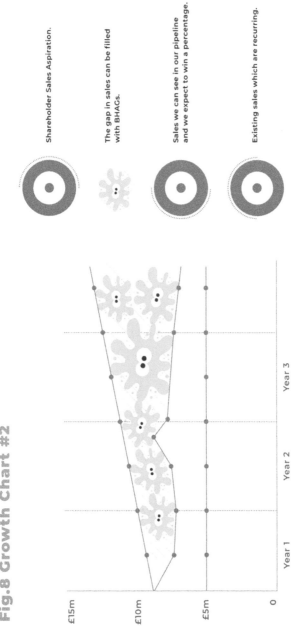

Fig.8 Growth Chart #2

Shareholder Sales Aspiration.

The gap in sales can be filled with BHAGs.

Sales we can see in our pipeline and we expect to win a percentage.

Existing sales which are recurring.

1. Consider the existing core business and downgrade the growth over the next three years to take account of contracts that may come to an end and day-to-day business that is lost. Your core business, if left untouched, unloved and un-innovated, will degrade and deteriorate over that three-year period. Show that deterioration. This is your core business (see Fig. 2).

2. Consider your pipeline – what new opportunities exist that you already know about? They may be new contracts you are already tracking, or prospects you have been building relationships and trust that turn into customers. What percentage of the pipeline do you think is going to fall to you? Take this percentage of potential wins and add these wins onto the graph. This is the additional income you can earn by exploiting your adjacent markets (see Fig. 3).

3. Look at the income gap created by the shareholders aspiration and identify your BHAGs. Plot these your potential wins into your business growth plan (see Fig. 4).

These three potential funding lines will form the basis of your business growth plan. Challenge yourself to take a long, hard look at your business as part of this business growth planning process. Take off the rose-tinted glasses, stop believing your own PR and expose your sales mind to the sense of peril that hangs over all good entrepreneurs. The world will move on, fashions and styles will change. What was yesterday's USP will be tomorrow's fish and chips. This cold review can benefit the business in many ways.

Sales teams will have a huge focus on sales for today, tomorrow and the end of the month. However, sales teams have a skill set focused on the short-term win. The team who develops opportunities for adjacent markets will have a disposition better suited to medium / long term goals. The BHAGs team will have real sense of independence and risk taking on high profile deals and these teams need separate focus meetings that will ensure they are not distracted by the work of the other teams. Establish separate meetings for each of the three layers of the growth plan:

- Defend the Core
- Develop Adjacent Markets
- Big Hairy Audacious Goals

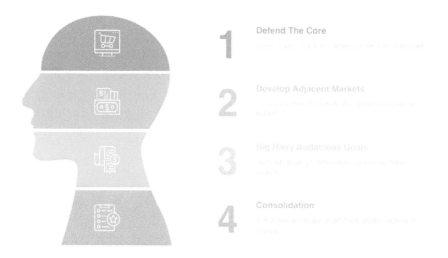

Defend the Core

This is a meeting with the sales team. It is to review the ongoing sales to existing customers and new customers within the existing sectors and networks. The focus here is to maintain and grow the existing accounts to defend the core business. Scientifically review all activity –

sales meetings, quotes, follow ups, conversion rates, face-to-face activity, referrals, awards won and post-mortems on all significant wins and losses – to ensure you learn and move forward. Hold the sales team accountable to hit the daily, weekly, monthly and annual sales targets. This role is about impacting the now and immediate future.

Adjacent Markets

This meeting is with the business development team. It is not about immediate sales, rather this meeting should focus on the medium-term opportunities to attract new customers and branch out into new sectors that nestle around the core business. The business development team must start by doing significant research to identify potential prospects. Once identified, relationship developments must follow to build long-term, trusting relationships. A takeaway from this relationship-building process is a full understanding of the prospect's pain points, the influencing network within the organisation and a clear pathway to a sales opportunity. Once established, this relationship can be handed over to a salesperson to complete and close out the sale. The business development team must report against a business development process (in the same way salespeople must report against a sales process).

Big Hairy Audacious Goals

This is a meeting with the big hairy audacious team and should focus on the larger, riskier projects requiring capital and significant resources. This team is largely made up of project managers. Each BHAG will require the appointment of a project leader their role is to take the feasibility study and bring it to life. They will have to be a strong, tenacious person because BHAG territory is often rough – you are treading a new path and encountering new problems for the first time. This meeting must focus on driving the outcomes from the project plan and challenging the process with a go/no go decision at key milestones. Remember – there is no shame in walking away from a project that has failed. There is shame is chucking good money after bad on a no hope 'ego' project.

Don't mix up the meetings, even if some people may populate all three teams. Be clear that sales is about what happens today and tomorrow. The development and pipeline team tracks what happens in the next 6–18 months. The strategic development and big hairy audacious goals team tracks what happens in the 18 months to four-year period. Establish a clear, steadfast and exceptional plan for each layer to deliver the targets offering individuals absolute support, while holding them clearly accountable.

One of my clients has followed this system to the letter and they are enjoying a clear pathway to doubling their business in the next 3 years. A clear plan has been developed, shared with all stakeholders and used to drive activity via simple visible KPIs. Year one of this plan has already produced fifty percent growth and a confident forward pipeline. The system works.

10 Golden Tips

1. Never start a growth trading period without a clear visual plan.
2. Clear your mind and get focused on the next 3-year trading period.
3. Consider the existing core business and degradation/growth.
4. Consider the pipeline – what can you see? What percentage will fall to you?
5. Look at the BHAGs and allocate timings and champions.
6. Review the activities to defend the core.
7. Review the piloting/prototype of adjacent markets.
8. Commit resources and leadership to BHAGs.
9. Establish separate meetings for each layer of the plan.
10. Establish a clear, steadfast expectation for each layer to deliver the targets.

KEY LEARNINGS

CHAPTER 7

1.

2.

3.

ACTION PLAN

CHAPTER 7

ACTION	WHO	PRIORITY	STATUS	NOTES	DUE DATE
1.					
2.					
3.					
4.					
5.					
6.					

8

ISLAND SWIMMING
· ·

So, you have set off to build this amazing, profitable business, but if you want staff, family and friends to come on this journey, you are going to have to ask people to embrace change. A major feature of your success will be to drive change as a leader of your business. The market and customer needs are changing with increasing pace. Therefore, agility to predict and respond to these shifting customer needs will determine your sustained success. Nothing stays constant in business. If you cannot change you cannot survive. The ability to change is critical. As much as we all profess to like and enjoy change, few of us really do.

Try this - put your hands front of you, clasp them together and interlock your fingers and thumbs as you would normally. Note which thumb is on the top. Then, separate your hands for a moment and do it again, only this time interlock them differently so that the other thumb is on top. You will notice it feels slightly awkward and uncomfortable and possibly took more time and concentration. All you have been asked you to do is to move five fingers ever so slightly, you will want to stick to the way that is comfortable. If this is how you feel just moving your fingers into a different place, then it is normal for all of us to feel awkward, uncomfortable and wary of doing our jobs in a different way. When you are driving your business to achieve accelerated growth and sustainable profits you are going to be asking lots of your staff and teams to do their jobs differently. This will cause resistance; it will feel uncomfortable for them, it will feel awkward for you and that is ok - it is normal. You are on a journey to change your business and so you must accept and acknowledge the impact this change will have on the team.

Leaving Paradise

Most of the time, no one really volunteers to change. Some of your staff may profess a willingness to embrace the change needed by the market, but deep down inside they are not willing to accept the potential risks of change.

Picture this: you have been shipwrecked on a deserted island in the middle of the ocean, surrounded by beautiful stone beaches, swaying palm trees, some fruit and blue cloudy skies. You would feel fortunate to be where you were. Sure, you might miss civilization, but you are at least comfortable and happy whilst you awaited a rescue. However, in the distance, about a mile away, you could see another beautiful deserted island with pristine sandy beaches, taller palm trees offering shade with coconuts, more exotic food, clearer blue skies and some boxes of provisions washed up from the shipwreck. Unfortunately, between the two islands, awaits a shoal of hungry sharks. Once you have seen the shoal of hungry sharks I suspect if I invited you to take a swim with me from your wonderful, but comfortable island to the other, slightly more wonderful island only a mile away, I suspect I may struggle to gain your commitment.

But what if I showed you a very active volcano on the island, that was rumbling, spewing hot molten lava and minutes away from a huge eruption? You may be more inclined to consider swimming to the other (slightly more wonderful) island. The journey might be treacherous as you wade into the surf. Luckily, you weave your way past each of the flesh-eating sharks safely. Then, in the last 20 yards, a shark makes a dive for your feet, but you manage to leap out of its way and drag yourself onto the beach with your bodies intact. Breathless but relieved, you stand on the beach of the new island, thankful for your safety and survival.

Settled into the new island, with everything you need, I suspect another suggestion of leaving the island to swim to another island would be met with a firm no, maybe even a laugh. Even equipped with a map that showed civilisation was nearby, you might avoid the risk and choose to wait for a ship to pass – after all, you had already risked everything once.

However, if I shared with you that your new island was home to thousands of venomous snakes, many of which you could see from the beach where you are standing, I suspect you may become much more inclined to take another risk if it meant surviving. The very real danger of staying on the second island, combined with the very real danger of going back to the first, just might give you the impetus to take a chance, build that raft and leave behind both islands in search of civilization.

This story highlights human nature. Your staff are human beings and we are programmed to find safety and stay there. There is only a very small percentage of the population who constantly look to move away from their comforts and seek risk: explorers, mountaineers and tightrope walkers. Your businesses are filled with team members who will naturally be inclined to avoid risk. Like most business owners, you seek to minimise risk for your greater benefit and your staff operate on exactly the same framework. Learning a new skill, taking on a new role, accepting additional responsibilities and agreeing to bigger targets should all sound like exciting opportunities. However, in many cases they spell the words; additional risk, opportunity to fail publicly and disappointment. In many cases your staff would prefer to stay where they are, safe and sound in their comfort zone, which is why you must perfect the leadership talent of highlighting the dangers of staying in comfort zones. You need to point out the potential impact of competitors and explain the changing economic conditions as it is important you help your teams understand that you are not suggesting change for change sake, but rather suggesting change to avoid, volcanos, hungry sharks and poisonous snakes. Your staff may not spot these dangers which is why they may be reluctant to change. As the leader of the business you have a responsibility to point out these dangers and thus facilitate successful change.

Change Isn't Comfortable

Asking anyone to make a change is always a tough request. Some people say they love change, but in reality, most people do not like the risk, upheaval and discomfort of change. If, therefore, you are to lead and inspire your teams to make an energetic leap into the unknown of change, you have to be able to convey verbally and passionately the dangers of staying where you are. Our teams may see the golden, inviting beaches on the new island, but they will also spot the hungry sharks and so will naturally feel a sense of reluctance to take this leap of faith. You will need to specifically point out the dangers of the smoking volcano and lava spewing and hurtling towards you and rolling down the sides of the mountains towards you and your team. In other words, if you want to engage your teams to look positively at change, you have to spell out the inherent dangers of staying where you are and maintaining the status quo. For example, maybe your logistics are out of date or your website does not serve your customers well. Maybe your customer service or product innovation has fallen by the wayside. No matter what the weak points are in your business, it is critical that you address them by making change and adapting to maintain your competitiveness. Each of these changes will require the full support of the teams in our businesses - we cannot expect this support for change unless we show them the erupting volcano. The ADKAR model below sets out a system for driving change.

ADKAR
CHANGE MANAGEMENT

AWARENESS	DESIRE	KNOWLEDGE	ABILITY	REINFORCEMENT
To create awareness of the need for change, you need everybody who is affected by it to be aware of the issues that triggered the initiative. That might mean sharing some uncomfortable truths, but people need understand the old way is no longer working.	To instil a desire for change, people need to know why it's good for them. For example, they might not care that the business's profits are low. But they will care if they know that low profitability may lead to the business freezing wage increases, having to implement layoffs, or even closing down.	There's no point in trying to implement change unless the people whose jobs are changing know how to get things done. Getting through this step could be as simple as showing them how you want them to work from now on and where they fit into the process flow. However, people might also need training.	When you implement a new process, you don't want to risk any "oops" moments. Hands-on training is the best training, and once people have demonstrated their ability, you can be reasonably confident that there won't be any costly errors later on.	During this stage, you should also be on the lookout for areas where the new process isn't serving you or is demotivating your staff. For instance, if you've overestimated a person or department's capacity and there's a bottleneck in the process, people will feel overworked and stressed out.

People Will Change When They Have To

You have to make sure that before you invite people to come on one of those dangerous journeys with you, you have painted explicitly the danger of staying where they are. Make sure that they can understand that the place where they are now, although comfortable and routine, will not be a comfortable and sustainable place to be in the future. Once you have painted that erupting volcano scenario clearly for them and they understand the unsustainability of staying where they are, they are more likely to gladly take that risk and join you.

The staff have to be able to see the risk, feel the vision and understand their role in it. You have to prove with facts and data that there is an erupting volcano, you cannot just ask them to take your word for it. The danger of the status quo has to be made personal. Staff will be motivated if you point out the danger for your company of staying on the island with the volcano, but they will be really motivated to get off the island if you can show them explicitly that the volcano holds real danger not just for the company but also for each member of the team because of the impact it could have on job security, salary and bonus levels, status, training or location. It is not about creating an atmosphere of fear, but rather sharing your knowledge of the position the business is in and aligning the future prospects for shareholders and staff with a forward-looking positive action plan for change. Remember, just clasping their hands together differently is not something that people enjoy doing, so asking them to do their job differently, take on more risks, lead entry into new markets and increasing the service levels will feel very uncomfortable for most of your team. But, change you must.

211°F or 212°F

Leaders have many issues on their mind, it is easy to forget the importance of boosting your team's energy. At 211°F water is hot but not boiling. Hot water is good for many things: washing your hands, having a shower and cleaning your cooking utensils. But hot water produces no steam, without steam - engines do not turn, they gather no speed. Without steam your business will be stationary and become stagnant. However, with 1 degree more passion, 1°F more energy from the leader the temperature of the water reaches 212°F – now we have steam. At 212°F your staff will sizzle, drive and stretch for excellence. At 212°F your business will produce the steam you need to drive the business turbines and smash through the glass ceiling.

The Ulrich model for employee connection (below) is a great visual which a leader can use to challenge themselves if their staff are not productive. If our staff are not being productive, we have to test the competence of our staff, test the attitudes of our staff and then ask ourselves the thorny question – are our staff finding their work meaningful. Any low scores on this test will result in low levels of productivity. Thankfully it is easy to find solutions once we have diagnosed the problem.

ULRICH'S STAGES OF EMPLOYEE CONNECTION

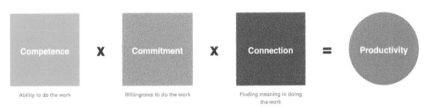

STAGES OF EMPLOYEE CONNECTION TO A BUSINESS

| Competence | X | Commitment | X | Connection | = | Productivity |

Ability to do the work   Willingness to do the work   Finding meaning in doing the work

Servant Led Leadership

Robert K. Greenleaf first coined the phrase "servant leadership" in his essay "The Servant as a Leader." In many ways like all ideas it is nothing new, but it is a framework I have readily adopted in my own business dealings. In essence I do not believe a dictatorial style of leadership will deliver sustainable results. I believe we need to be approachable and encourage our staff feel comfortable about approaching leaders with their issues so that the leader and the member of staff can work together to solve problems. This open democratic style increases communication and will boost staff motivation.

10 Golden Tips

1. If friends, family and staff want to come with you on your journey, they have to be willing to embrace change.
2. Asking someone to embrace change is a tough request, make it strategically.
3. No one volunteers to swim through shark-infested waters unless they know there is no other escape route off the island.
4. Once safe, no one volunteers to venture out into the unknown on a raft unless there is something very valuable that they are determined to find.
5. Your staff won't want to take that swim through the shark-infested waters, it is critical for the leaders to motivate, encourage and inspire their teams to grasp these changes and the necessity for them.
6. You have to understand that your staff will rarely commit to change unless they are on a burning platform.
7. You have to paint a picture of the justification for change (i.e. the burning platform).

8. The staff have to be able to see a better future and their role within it, or they will not want to come with you on your journey.

9. You have to use facts and data to show the danger at hand for all stakeholders to prove the burning platform and highlight that it creates danger for the company, shareholders, managers and all staff.

10. Change is uncomfortable, but necessary.

KEY LEARNINGS

CHAPTER 8

1.

2.

3.

ACTION PLAN
CHAPTER 8

ACTION	WHO	PRIORITY	STATUS	NOTES	DUE DATE
1.					
2.					
3.					
4.					
5.					
6.					

9

ACCOUNTABILITY

· · · · · · · · · · · · · · · · · · · ·

A quick recap. If you want to grow the business, you will need a plan. The plan must have clear, smart objectives and KPIs. These KPIs must be allocated to specific individuals and reviewed on a regular basis. This process of allocating KPIs and reviewing them on a regular basis provides a framework for accountability. Each stage in the accountability framework is important and must be followed with due care and attention. Holding ourselves and others accountable sounds easy, but nothing could be further from the truth.

There is No Such Thing as Perfect

Holding ourselves and each other accountable is really tough. People rarely invite accountability, we don't even like holding ourselves accountable. If we did, we would all be living perfect lives. Never speeding, overeating, over drinking, never taking too many risks, always cutting the grass, always living in a perfectly clean house and never walking on the cracks in the pavement. Life would be much better if we never said a rough word, never fell out with anybody, or failed an exam – but life is not like that. Maybe there are some perfect people out there, but I think they are a rare breed. Most of us struggle, at some point and at some level with holding ourselves accountable and sadly, we can't even hold each other accountable without it leading to rancour, disappointment, frustration or an argument. If we can't hold ourselves accountable and we cannot hold each other accountable, it can be very difficult to achieve anything.

Accountability is Critical to Success

If you are going to hold yourself accountable, you have to set clear expectations about what you expect. You need to check that the team, or individuals, have the resources necessary to complete their task. You have to make sure that they have the skills and talents to enable them to complete the task and do it comfortably with their skillset. You also have to ensure that they are clear about what good looks like - you cannot ask someone to do something better if you have never given them the opportunity to see what better looks like. Get out, see your competitors, travel, read, explore, meet people, talk to them and find out what good looks like. Only when you have shown them this vision of what good looks like can you take steps towards a good outcome. As part of the accountability framework you can utilise this shared sense of what good looks like to support and challenge progress, but you have to make sure that you have cleared all the barriers out of the way. If something has not been done before, it is very likely that something has prevented the successful achievement: a person, internal politics, poor teamwork or some rigmarole. You, therefore, have a responsibility to not allow this failure to sit at your door – as their leader, remove all barriers to prevent this from happening.

To track accountability, you have to set up ongoing monitoring and reporting structures, which are driven by the individuals delivering on the project. Let them report to themselves and then report to you. It is no good if the leader just approaches the team with a set of data that proves the team is failing or has not achieved the objective. Instead give the team the opportunity to see the data first so that they can approach you - perhaps with their failed performance, but also with their solutions and ideas as to how they are going to make it more successful in the future. All the feedback has to be attributable to individuals as well as teams. It is fine having a team that is responsible for delivering an objective, you can set up team accountability structures, but you also have to have the names of individuals who carry the burden of achieving success, so that whether something goes right, or something goes wrong, you know exactly who to speak to.

Patrick Lencioni wrote a classic book about teams called Dysfunctional Teams. In the book he relates the five characteristics of dysfunctional teams:

- Absence of Trust
- Fear of Conflict
- Lack of Commitment
- Avoidance of Accountability
- Inattention to Results

It can be quite sobering to relate this text to your business. I have never seen a successful business which could be characterized by these five themes. Leaders must bring their staff together to work in aligned functional teams who are inspired to reach for the stars. The world is full of very competent competitors. Our staff give us the biggest opportunity to stay ahead of the crowd and distinguish ourselves through excellence. The dashboard below is used by a company responsible to deliver audits around the world and this visual pulls the team activity together on a single page.

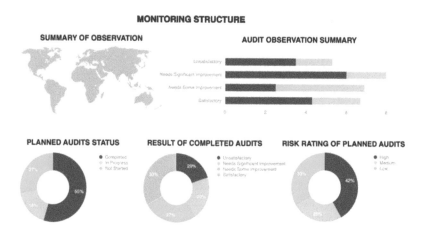

Be a Strong Leader and Support Progress

This is not about bullying, intimidation or a blame game, this is just about making sure that individuals know they are being held accountable to the whole team, the company and themselves for the delivery of significant parts of a project. You are in a position to hold yourselves and the individuals in your teams accountable, so set clear expectations. You have got the resources that they need to complete the task, they have got skills and talents to be able to do it. They understand what good looks like. You have taken away barriers and put in reporting and monitoring systems for them to drive and report on. You have got visual and transparent feedback and all individuals involved in the project understand their part and responsibility. Now you can look forward to holding yourself and your team accountable. At all times leaders need to use their emotional intelligence to make the right inputs at the right time to the right individuals and teams. One size leadership does not fit all the scenarios you will face as a leader. Invest in yourself to enhance your understanding of your emotional leadership style and how to boost this asset to drive accelerated growth which is sustainable.

10 Golden Tips

1. Holding ourselves and each other accountable is really tough.
2. You cannot hold your teams accountable unless you have set clear expectations.
3. You have to check that your team has the resources necessary to complete the task.
4. You have to make sure that your team has the skills necessary to complete the task.
5. You have to ensure that your team is clear about what 'good' looks like before you expect them to do better.
6. You have to remove barriers in order for your staff to succeed.
7. You have to set up ongoing monitoring and reporting structures to hold your teams accountable.
8. The reporting needs to be visual and transparent to make improvement possible.
9. All feedback has to be attributable to individuals as well as teams.
10. Once you are in a position to hold yourselves, individuals and teams accountable, you can make critical changes and improvements to support progress.

KEY LEARNINGS

CHAPTER 9

1.

2.

3.

ACTION PLAN

CHAPTER 9

ACTION	WHO	PRIORITY	STATUS	NOTES	DUE DATE
1.					
2.					
3.					
4.					
5.					
6.					

10

PIPELINE
• • • • • • • • • • •

A sales pipeline is simply a list of potential sales opportunities recorded from the earliest stage all the way through to conclusion.

Sales are History

Sales reports and sales data are about merely historical records by the time the reports arrive, you can study the data but what they report has already happened. There is nothing you can do to impact or change it. The only hope to affect future sales is to build, nurture, align and look after your pipeline. Sales reports are worth looking at, but do not fall into the trap of obsessively studying sales reports, because this is as a distraction to getting out and selling. The pipeline records the potential of the future, this is where your real value will be. The size of your pipeline is the best forecaster for the size of your future sales.

Develop Your Own Unique Sales Process

To develop your sales, you have to have a sales process. Understand each of the five, seven or twelve key steps in your sales process. Write them down and record each of your prospects at the relevant stage in your sales process. Fig. 9 is a generic example of a sales pipeline I created – every sales pipeline will be unique to the business. The sales process shows the key stages for the sale opportunity to pass through, from left to right. Each opportunity is managed through each stage of the process until you either achieve a sale or fail. It is important to record this in your systems as a success or fail. The data collected from this process will highlight where the leaks in your sales process are and highlight the actions needed to be taken to both reduce the leaks and enable more sales opportunities to progress to a successful sale. Good lead generation will be the lifeblood of your business growth. There are many ways to develop good quality leads: referrals, trusted advisor status, blogs, social media, networking, platforms for public speaking and promotions. Even with these good methods deployed lead generation is still a numbers game. Activity drives leads.

Study Your Sales Pipeline

The value of your pipeline in the 'Opportunity' column should be divided by the amount of sales achieved. This calculation will give you a conversion rate and this conversion rate will highlight the effectiveness of your sales process. Small tweaks in your sales process can improve

STAGE OF SALES PROCESS	TOTAL VALUE	OPPORTUNITY SPOTTED	CONTACT MADE	QUALIFIED	INFO SENT	VISITED	NEGOTIATE	SALE
VALUE OF OPPORTUNITY		5%	5%	20%	20%	35%	45%	70%
SMITH BROS.	100k		5000					
JONES LIMITED	50k					17,500		
POLLARD & PARTNERS	210k						94,500	
DEGRADED VALUE OF THE PIPELINE	117,000							

your conversion rate and result in a big impact on the sales secured. Your pipeline should show many prospects and the total under each column can be added together to give you an understanding of the value at each stage of the sales process.

Fig. 9 reflects the key stages in this example sales process. The percentages show the value of each deal which can be conservatively added together to give a total pipeline value. For example: in Fig. 9, only 5% of the total value for new opportunities is included in total value of the pipeline. This is because many opportunities will drop out at each stage of the sales process. It would be cavalier to take 100% of the value of all the opportunities to the total pipeline value. This would overstate the likely future sales achieved. Even at the point of sales, I would recommend taking only 70% of the value of the sale, as it can still be cancelled, or the customer may be unable to fulfil the obligation they have entered into with your company.

It is also possible to enter a notional time it takes to travel between each stage of the process on the sales process. This helps to highlight opportunities that have become stuck at a particular stage of the sales process and would benefit from further follow up.

Focus on Conversion Rates

If you are aiming for £5m of sales and your conversion rate is 20% (i.e. you manage to secure 20% of the initial opportunities qualified), then you are going to need a pipeline of £25m to feed your sales for the following year. If, however, you have a sales target of £5m and you have £3m of returning 'core business', then you only need to seek £2m of new business. If your conversion rate is still 20% the total of your sales

STAGE	REVIEW MARKET	IDENTIFY PROSPECTS	IDENTIFY INFLUENCERS	UNDERTAKE MARKET RESEARCH	DEVELOP CONCEPTUAL PROPOSAL	SECURE INTEREST FROM PROSPECT	HANDOVER TO SALES
JOHNSONS		***					
DONALD PARTNERS				***			
PHILIPS			***				
SIMPSPONS					***		

pipeline will need to be £10m. Many business owners underestimate the size of the pipeline that will be needed to fuel the following year's sales target and many will not even be aware of their conversion rate. It is worth noting in the example given above that if the conversion rate drops to 10%, the pipeline now needs to exceed £50m to fuel the same £5m worth of sales. Conversely, if the conversion can improve from 20% to 40%, the sales pipeline now only needs to be £12.5m. As you can see, working on your conversion rate can have a dramatic impact on your lead generation. Better conversion means less wasted lead generation.

Understand Your Business Development Process

Business development means different things to different people. I have always judged business development as the process of identifying larger, longer term, more strategic business opportunities. Business development staff are usually working 1 – 2 years ahead of the business opportunity being ready to pass over to the sales team. It is difficult when you try to validate the investment in business development because much of this work is conceptual and is focused on building long-term relationships. However, you will be able to establish a business development process. This business development process should set out each stage in the business development activity. You need to understand how you go from identifying a longer-term opportunity which you nurture to all the way through building trust with a prospect. Establish your business development pipeline then track all your business development deals through this process. A business development process may include these stages:

- Review your existing markets
- Identify large companies within your sector who are not yet your customers
- Study new markets
- Review the mid-term economic analysis to spot growth areas
- Understand the behaviors and intentions of your competitors
- Short list your prospects
- Innovate new solutions to meet the pain points of your prospects
- Contact and engage prospects
- Undertake detailed research of prospects and refine solutions to their pain points
- Review your businesses capability and enhance your USPs to attract the prospects
- Develop refined proposals for your prospects
- Engage your sales team to hand over the oven ready prospects.

It is important to review the business development pipeline with the business development staff to track and evaluate this investment.

Study Your Business Development Pipeline

Fig. 10 gives you a generic example of a business development pipeline. The stages of a business development pipeline are different from the sales process pipeline because business development opportunities are more long-term and require much more significant research and relationship building. The second row of the business development pipeline gives you the chance to list all of the business development opportunities you are focusing on, with each opportunity needing its own row. The final row in Fig. 10 reflects the size of the market opportunity you are focusing on. Market research will form a significant part of identifying your business development opportunities. Market research is a serious business, it not just a matter of asking prospects if they will be interested in your products or services. Rather it the use of tools and techniques to discern a potential market need in a level of verifiable detail which enables you to make investment decisions. The design of questionnaires is a fine art and you would benefit greatly from the input of experts. The outcome of the market research should allow prototype products or services to be developed which can be piloted and tested to allow for further refinement, prior to launch or cancellation.

Don't Overstate the Value of Your Pipelines

In both your sales and business development pipelines, it is important to degrade these opportunities at every stage of the process so that you do not overstate the value of your pipeline. Put all sales opportunities into the start of the pipeline. For example, if you see a crane go up, or you hear a restaurant opening, or you hear of a supplier that is closing down, this may be the start of a new niche and a new opportunity, so note it down to follow up. But, do not record 100% of the potential sale value, otherwise you are going to end up with a pipeline that has a value of several hundred million and often delivers very sourly on that potential. Perhaps only take 5% of the value of all new opportunities, or 10% of those opportunities that have been validated. There is no point putting in 100% of the potential sales value for each opportunity into the pipeline as this will inflate the potential sales total. The problem in inflating the sales pipeline is that it will deflate very quickly in the final stages. Therefore, I suggest taking a very conservative approach where you only take a reduced % of the value for each sales opportunity into consideration. For example, when a new opportunity is introduced into the pipeline, I would suggest only taking 5% of the potential opportunity into consideration. This can increase from taking 5% of an early stage opportunity building up perhaps 70% for a deal in the final stages of negotiation. This staged process of managing potential deals through towards a sale and only taking a conservative % of the value for each deal to an overall considered sum will ensure you do not overstate the value of your future deals.

Don't Forget to Follow Up

A follow up is the best friend a pipeline can ever have. Follow up, follow up, follow up. Nurture, develop, maintain contact and improve trust. Ensuring this will bring that sale closer to you all the time. Use data and analysis to record the leaks that you have got in your pipeline and repair these leaks - if you don't, these leaks will reduce your final conversion rate. So, if you have 100% of the ideas in the first stage of the business sales process and you end up with only converting 25% of those sales opportunities, where did you lose the other 75% of potential opportunities? Make sure you undertake post-mortems in detail (we have talked about these in the previous chapter) analyse and understand why you are losing opportunities out of your pipeline. Learn from these post-mortems and implement changes to your future sales, business development and pipeline management.

10 Golden Tips

1. Your sales are history by the time they are reported
2. The only hope for the future is your pipeline.
3. The sales pipeline records the future and is your real value.
4. Develop your sales process.
5. Develop your business development process.
6. Develop your strategic sales pipeline.
7. Identify every opportunity and track through to sale or fail.
8. Degrade all your opportunities at each stage of the process so you do not overstate the value of your pipeline.
9. A follow up is the best friend a pipeline ever had.
10. Record the leaks in your pipeline to improve your final conversion rate.

KEY LEARNINGS

CHAPTER 10

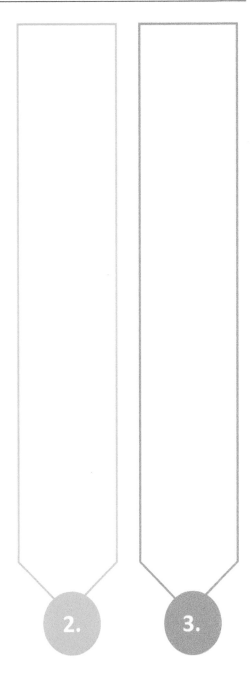

ACTION PLAN

CHAPTER 10

ACTION	WHO	PRIORITY	STATUS	NOTES	DUE DATE
1.					
2.					
3.					
4.					
5.					
6.					

11

YOUR ENERGY PLAN

The only thing that makes "things" happen is energy. You can't light a bulb, drive a car, enjoy your air conditioning, watch TV, or listen to music without energy and it is true to say you cannot build relationships, run a business, or make sales without buckets of energy. I have never seen a successful business that did not have buckets of energy. The leader of the business must have huge amounts of energy to drive the business, set the vision, implement the plan and continually inspire, nurture, challenge, stretch and celebrate the staff.

Feed Your Soul

Leadership is a tough, relentless job. A leader who puts their heart and soul into inspiring their teams will inevitably have days when they feel ground down. A leader of the business therefore must have ways to replenish their energy because their energy is the energy source for their business. So, if the energy of the leader drains or dims, the whole team can suffer. It is critical for leaders to have a toolkit of resources to dip into at times when energy levels dip into the red. My advice is to write out your own personal list of resources that boost your energy. List the foods: chicken soup, ice cream and list the drinks: the fancy sparkling mineral water with freshly squeezed lemon juice in it, orange juice (with bits in it), ice cold elderflower water. List the music that makes you bounce, the walks or exercises that fill you with energy, the books that refresh your spirit, the poems that revisit happy memories, the picture is that inspire you and the smells that fuel your soul.

Three Types of People

In my 40 years of business I have met many people and I have identified that they fall into three main types of people. There are drainers, radiators and sustainers. The drainers are those people who take every ounce of your energy that you have in your bones. They have a problem for every solution and when you leave their company you feel weary. Having spent time with them, you walk away a former shadow of yourself.

Radiators, however, are a joy – the complete opposite of drainers. Radiators draw people to them. They make your heart sing, lift your soul and make everything feel exciting. They radiate energy and boost yours – they make every mountain seem climbable. Radiators lift and inspire their teams. They make constant eye contact with people with whom they are engaging. Radiators make you feel special and taller than before you met them.

It is not to say radiators do not have bad days or go through difficult periods in their lives, but they are more likely to find support structures and move through hardships without dragging others under with them.

Sustainers are the middle ground and can take an idea and go with it, putting in the necessary time and effort day after day to keep the project and energy going. They might not bring a ton of energy to the scene, but they won't suck up a ton of energy either, as long as they have the proper support, training and skill sets to do the job right. Sustainers have the steadiness to keep plugging away and doing what needs to be done, even after the initial excitement of a new venture wears off.

Be a Radiator

Put a list in the back of your daily journal of those things that help you maintain and boost your energy. As I said above, list the food, the drinks, the walks, the books, the pictures, the smells, but also the people who bring you joy and instill you with energy. Adore and keep close to the radiators in your life. Equip the sustainers with the tools they need to succeed and then sit back while they keep the energy moving day in and day out. Limit your time with those who drain. Most of all, if you want to be a successful business leader, you must be a radiator at home and with friends – not just in your business. It might be difficult to be a constant source of energy and inspiration, but this is your job and this is what your energy list is for. Leaders sometimes ask me, "Why do I need to write out a list of energy boosters and put it in the back of my daily journal?" I explain that when a leader is full of drive and bouncing with energy, they don't need a list. But when a leader does get run down, when their energy levels hit red and they realise they need to top up, they cannot even begin to remember how to go about filling up their energy and they need something visual to guide them back to their energy source. The same goes for you – when you are low on energy, you lose the ability to know how to top up the energy. So, write the list now, while you are in a good place and store the list in an accessible place for when you need it.

Radiators are always surrounded by people who want to be close to draw off their energy. Make sure wherever you are that you see people drawn to be close to you so that they can feed off your energy and inspiration. This is when you know you are a radiator.

If you find yourself in a room alone, maybe you are a drain. Shake yourself, use that energy list and become the radiator your business needs you to be.

10 Golden Tips

1. Buckets of energy are necessary for a successful business. No energy = no success.
2. The leader of the business must have huge amounts of energy.
3. The leader of the business must have ways to replenish their energy.
4. Write out your own personal list of resources that boost your energy. List the foods, the drinks, the music, the walks, the books, the poems, the pictures, the smells and the words that refuel your soul.
5. Put your list in the back of your daily journal, diary, or task list so that it is there for you when you need that energy boost.
6. List people in three columns; Drainers, Sustainers and Radiators. Drainers take every ounce of your energy and drop it down the sewer. Sustainers do not bring a lot of energy to the room but can keep energy flowing day in and day out. Radiators makes your heart sing, lift your soul and make you feel like every mountain is climbable.

7. Stay away from the drains.
8. Adore and keep close to the radiators in your life.
9. Equip the sustainers with tools to help them succeed so they can sustain critical processes.
10. Be a radiator in your business as well as at home and with friends.

KEY LEARNINGS

CHAPTER 11

1.

2.

3.

ACTION PLAN
CHAPTER 11

ACTION	WHO	PRIORITY	STATUS	NOTES	DUE DATE
1.					
2.					
3.					
4.					
5.					
6.					

12

ACTION PLAN

• • • • • • • • • • • • • • • •

W_e know if you do not plan to succeed you are planning to
fail. So, the final critical stage is to pull together all the plans
in this book from the end of each chapter and develop them
into one single plan for your business. Identify all the actions from the
previous chapters, list your actions, times, dates, people and numbers,
numbers, numbers. You need to know when you are getting closer to
your planned outcomes so you can monitor your movements – e.g. if
you are stagnant or drifting – and when you have arrived at your final
destination. Study the choreography required to ensure first things first
and make sure the list of actions that you are going to do are in the
correct order. Make sure that you have validated your ideas before you
invest time and money and ensure the activities are planned in a way
that will make the most of the resources and investment so you can
achieve the best possible result. Make sure that you have got your service
right. Allocate every action to a single person, not so that you can blame

them later, but because actions identified and allocated to individuals with their names on them are much more likely to be achieved. Agree on critical deadlines and milestones and be clear where you want to be by a particular time – not just at the end of the journey.

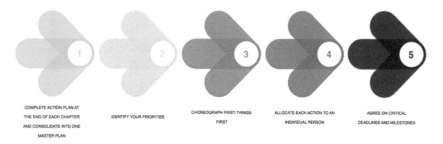

COMPLETE ACTION PLAN AT
THE END OF EACH CHAPTER
AND CONSOLIDATE INTO ONE
MASTER PLAN

IDENTIFY YOUR PRIORITIES

CHOREOGRAPH FIRST-THINGS-
FIRST

ALLOCATE EACH ACTION TO AN
INDIVIDUAL PERSON

AGREE ON CRITICAL
DEADLINES AND MILESTONES

Don't Be Afraid to Act

Be clear in the action plan; plan what key outcomes you want to achieve at key milestones. If you are faced with an action plan that fails to achieve key outcomes by the milestone date, be proactive in either changing the plan or stopping the project. Changing the plan, or stopping the project, are both positive ways forward. Failure only comes when you fail to act on a report that highlights a failure. Lack of action leads to misery.

If the project is cancelled, you can then utilise your findings and recycle your idea, its money and your learning to make more success of future plans and ideas. Agree to simple, clear outcomes with numbers. Test your idea to confirm your action plan will be watertight, realistic and will deliver the objectives and outcomes that you have set yourself. Make the plans visual to all staff and undertake full briefings to ensure total company ownership of the plan. You cannot achieve anything that is amazing on your own, you have to ensure that you take all the best people with you. Brief the whole company, ensure understanding, discuss the plan, debate it, disagree with it, align yourselves, review it and change the plan. Once you have got the final plan you are ready to start.

Adapt Your Plan and Celebrate Success

Report growth progress daily on a company wide basis. Make sure you know exactly how many steps you have taken in the plan and how your growth correlates with your targets. Report how many visits, quotes, follow ups and face-to-face meetings you have had. Track how many calls you have made, hits and interest you have generated from social media, webinars and seminars people are responding to, customers you have got signed up and successful projects you are delivering. Make these details clear to everybody in the business so they too can track and enjoy the success, or change and adapt to suit the circumstances you find ourselves in. Use feedback to tweak your plan and celebrate its success.

You really do have to celebrate success. It is a tough, difficult journey you are setting out on and you are taking people on a mountain climb every day of the week. So, when you achieve your objectives and plant the flag at the top of the mountain, you have to make sure that you are as good at celebrating success as you are at driving the team to achieve it. When you have a success worth celebrating, get the BBQ out, order two dozen doughnuts, light a candle and enjoy the success. Celebration and success will fuel the motivation and energy you are all going to need to climb the next mountain, which starts tomorrow. If you follow this system you will be able to track your success.

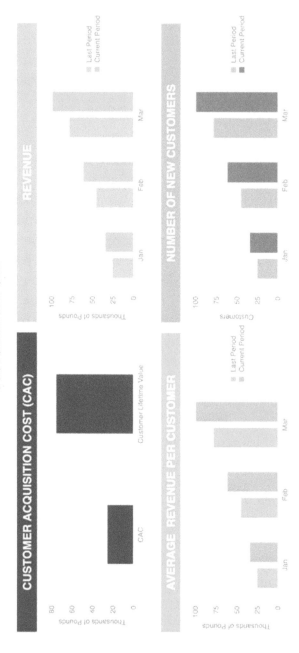

10 Golden Tips

1. Audit your plans and identify all actions
2. List your actions.
3. Study the choreography required to ensure 'first things first.'
4. Allocate every action to one single person.
5. Agree on critical deadlines and milestones.
6. Agree on clear simple outcomes.
7. Test to confirm your plan will 100% deliver the outcomes required.
8. Make plans visual to all staff and undertake full briefings to ensure total company ownership.
9. Report growth progress daily, companywide.
10. Tweak plans based on feedback and celebrate success.

So well done for getting this far, you have made it. You have studied my system, actioned 120 golden tips, highlighted 36 key learning points, committed to 72 actions and now you are ready to make it happen. Now you are ready to execute your plan.

Thank you and good luck. Keep me in your loop and tell me about your successes.

Thanks

Roy Newey

KEY LEARNINGS

CHAPTER 12

ACTION PLAN

CHAPTER 12

ACTION	WHO	PRIORITY	STATUS	NOTES	DUE DATE
1.					
2.					
3.					
4.					
5.					
6.					

Lightning Source UK Ltd.
Milton Keynes UK
UKHW021155101220
374911UK00008B/516